TRAFFIC AND THE POLICE

A publication of the Joint Center for Urban Studies
of the Massachusetts Institute of Technology
and Harvard University

TRAFFIC AND THE POLICE

Variations in Law-Enforcement Policy

John A. Gardiner

Harvard University Press

Cambridge, Massachusetts

1969

TO MOLLY

Acknowledgments

The research on which this study is based was begun while I was a V. O. Key, Jr., Fellow of the Joint Center for Urban Studies of the Massachusetts Institute of Technology and Harvard University, and a dissertation fellow of the Woodrow Wilson National Fellowship Foundation. I also gratefully acknowledge research support from the University of Wisconsin Faculty Research Committee and the Russell Sage Foundation Program in Sociology and Law at the University of Wisconsin. Computer time at Harvard and the University of Wisconsin was supported by the National Science Foundation. I wish to thank Bruce Campbell of the Massachusetts Safety Council, the personnel of the Massachusetts Registry of Motor Vehicles, and the more than five hundred police chiefs who so willingly provided the data used in this book.

My thanks for jobs well done to Florence Berger, Jean Billingsley, Keith Billingsley, Deborah Carpenter, Richard Collins, Margaret A. Jones, and Joel Margolis, who labored faithfully over the collection and analysis of data. Valuable comments and suggestions on earlier drafts of this work were offered by Rufus P. Browning, Jr., James W. Davis, Jr., Kenneth Dolbeare, Herman Goldstein, Herbert Jacob, Michael Lipsky, Donald J. McCrone, and Neil Milner.

Finally, I must gratefully acknowledge the advice and encouragement of James Q. Wilson of the Harvard Department of Government. All responsibility for errors and abuse of this advice remains, of course, with the author.

Portions of this study were previously presented in different form as a paper at the 1966 annual meeting of the American Political Science Association, subsequently published in James Q. Wilson, ed., *City Politics and Public Policy* (New York: John Wiley, 1968).

J.A.G.

Stony Brook, New York
September 1968

Contents

Tables

TRAFFIC AND THE POLICE

Introduction: Variations in Traffic-Law Enforcement

Throughout the 1960s, public interest has increasingly been directed toward the activities of police departments. On the one hand, studies such as the 1967 Report[1] of the National Crime Commission have questioned the technical capacity of local police forces to cope with riots, organized crime, and the apparent (although not unquestioned[2]) increase in urban crime rates. On the other hand, civil-liberties groups have been decrying the inability or disinclination of the police to change their arrest and interrogation procedures, following recent Supreme Court decisions; and community-relations groups have been asking whether policemen are adequately trained and motivated to deal with complex and delicate minority-group problems.

1. President's Commission on Law Enforcement and Administration of Justice, *The Challenge of Crime in a Free Society,* and *Task Force Report: The Police* (Washington: Government Printing Office, 1967).

2. See Ronald H. Beattie, "Problems of Criminal Statistics in the United States," *Journal of Criminal Law, Criminology, and Police Science,* XLVI (July–August 1955), 178–186; Institute of Public Administration, *Crime Records in Police Management* (New York: Institute of Public Administration, 1952); Marvin E. Wolfgang, "Uniform Crime Reports: A Critical Appraisal," *University of Pennsylvania Law Review,* CXI (April 1963), 708–738; James Q. Wilson, "Crime in the Streets," *The Public Interest,* no. 5 (Fall 1966), 26–35. For an illustration of the results following a change in police crime-reporting policies, see Eric Pace, " 'True' City Tally of Crime Pushes Rates Up Sharply," *New York Times,* April 5, 1966. For a longitudinal study of crime rates in one city, see Theodore N. Ferdinand, "The Criminal Patterns of Boston since 1849," *American Journal of Sociology,* LXXIII (July 1967), 84–99.

As the importance and complexity of police responsibilities have become more apparent to the general public, social scientists are turning their attention to the behavior of law-enforcement personnel and institutions. Sociologists and political scientists have begun to study police-recruitment patterns,[3] attitudes toward the public, and organizational norms, in order to explain how policemen perceive their roles and environment.[4] On another level, there are studies of relations between the police and the community as a whole, public views of law-enforcement institutions, and desired levels of the enforcement of particular laws.[5] Finally, a number of scholars have argued that the activities of police departments must be studied in an "opportunity cost" framework, pointing out that police decisionmaking takes place within a context of limited resources, a context in which the men and other resources of a department must be distributed among an incredible variety of regulatory and service functions required by the community.[6]

3. See, e.g., James Q. Wilson, "Generational and Ethnic Differences among Career Police Officers," *American Journal of Sociology*, LXIX (March 1964), 522–528.

4. James Q. Wilson, "Police Morale, Reform, and Citizen Respect: The Chicago Case," in David J. Bordua, ed., *The Police: Six Sociological Essays* (New York: Wiley, 1967); Michael Banton, *The Policeman in the Community* (London: Tavistock, 1964); Jerome Skolnick, *Justice without Trial: Law Enforcement in Democratic Society* (New York: Wiley, 1966).

5. See Banton, *The Policeman in the Community*; Robert W. Hodge, "The Public, the Police, and the Administration of Justice" (Chicago: National Opinion Research Center, 1965, mimeo); and the articles on public attitudes toward law enforcement, gambling, and corruption in the November 1967 issue of the *Annals*.

6. See, e.g., Herman Goldstein, "Police Discretion: The Ideal versus the Real," *Public Administration Review*, XXIII (September 1963), 140–148; Wayne R. LaFave, *Arrest: The Decision To Take a Suspect into Custody* (Boston: Little, Brown, 1966); and President's Commission on Law Enforcement and Administration of Justice, *Task Force Report: The Police,*

Whereas most of the public interest in the role of the police has been directed toward problems of *clear* violations of the law (murders, riots, the activities of crime syndicates),[7] many of the most interesting questions about police activities are in that large "gray area" existing between patterns of conduct which are clearly accepted by the society and those which are clearly condemned. Should the police break up a friendly poker game? Is prostitution a matter for police intervention or for the individual conscience? Are traffic-law violations worth bothering about if they do not threaten public safety? From the point of view of the public, police decisions on these questions are important factors in delineating the boundaries between the social values of liberty and order or security. From the point of view of the police, the need to make decisions within this limited area challenges the strength of the policeman's commitment to the public expectation that all laws will be literally enforced, and also strains the public's support for the police in more serious matters.

To a significant extent, a general understanding of the activities of local police departments can be gained through a study of law enforcement in these gray areas: areas of regulation in which neither the police department nor individual officers are given clear instructions by the public or its lawmaking institutions. Free from (or unaided by) either a clear public mandate or regular scrutiny by the press, interest groups, bar associations, and the judiciary—most defendants in vice or traffic cases plead guilty and do not seek the advice of attorneys—the critical decisions on the direction and level of enforcement of these regula-

---

ch. 2, "Law Enforcement Policy: The Police Role." For a useful bibliography of the major social science literature on the police, see Bordua, pp. 253–258.

7. See Hodge, "The Public, the Police, and the Administration of Justice."

tions are made within the police department, often by the individual policeman who is faced with an immediate decision whether to arrest, warn, or ignore an observed violator.

One of the most important of these areas of police work is the enforcement of laws regulating moving traffic—speeding, stop signs, traffic lights, and so forth. It is generally believed (at least by safety and police organizations) that traffic-law enforcement promotes safety, thereby decreasing fatalities, injuries, and insurance costs. For the policeman, depending upon his assignment, traffic-law enforcement is important in a different sense—it is either a full-time task or else one of several functions to be performed in the course of his routine patrol of the city.

For both the community and the police, traffic-law enforcement constitutes an important area of regulation, but the instructions that the community gives its policemen are somewhat sparse. The formal laws are, of course, clear: "No automobile shall be driven at a rate of speed greater than 30 m.p.h. in a thickly settled district"; "Every automobile shall come to a full stop at a stop sign"; and so on. The traffic officer has a series of tools with which to enforce these laws: he can merely stop violators and give them a lecture, write a warning that will become part of the motorist's record, or, finally, bring violators into court. The laws do not, however, tell the police how much time to devote to traffic, whether to enforce laws strictly or loosely, or which sanction should be applied in what situation; there is an unwritten assumption that *all* violators will be arrested and that discretion in punishment will be exercised by the judge rather than the policeman.

The assumption behind the formal traffic law that every violator will be apprehended and arrested cannot be satisfied by any police force. Limited resources and a multitude of other police duties, if nothing else, make it impossible. Any officer assigned to traffic work can only patrol a limited area for a limited number of hours, and the assignment of an officer to traffic work means that he will be unavailable for vice, homicide, or burglary investigations. If this appraisal of the capacities of our police forces is correct, then the relevant questions for the analyst of the police become: *How much* traffic-law enforcement? What *degree* of violation of the laws will lead to police action? What *proportion* of a police department's resources will be directed toward traffic enforcement rather than some other duty? What is the *effective* level of enforcement in the community?

In trying to measure the effective rate at which the police enforce traffic laws in American cities, we face a major methodological problem. If we knew how many violations had actually been committed in each city and town, we could say that *x* percent of all violations committed in City A led to tickets, *y* percent in B, and so forth. In most areas of law enforcement, we cannot fill this data gap by assuming equality (say by assuming that every city sees a similar number of each type of offense per thousand people) and then concluding that variations in the number of arrests are a "measure" of variations in police policy. FBI figures on offenses known to the police, while of questionable accuracy,[8] indicate that there are substantial differences in the crime rates of different cities. In the area of traffic-law violation, however, an assumption of equality might not be so tenuous. It seems somewhat more reasonable to assume that drivers in every city in the country have an equal propensity to speed or coast through stop signs than it would be to assume a constant rate of burglary or prostitution.

8. See the sources cited in note 2 above.

Before discussing the legitimacy of this assumption of equal rates, let us examine some data derived from it. First, as indicators of the traffic-enforcement activities of local police departments, we can use the number of moving-traffic tickets written in 1964 by 508 police forces in cities with populations (in 1960) greater than 25,000.[9] Second, to standardize these figures by some estimate of the volume of traffic in the city (and thus, by hypothesis, of the volume of actual traffic violations), the number of tickets written can be divided by the number of motor vehicles registered in that city in 1964 and by the city's population. Since my study focuses upon the role of the police, the number of tickets written has also been divided by the number of full-time policemen (excluding clerical and maintenance workers) on the police force. The distribution of responses on each of the three measures are presented in Tables 1, 2, and 3.

Put in words, looking at only one of these measures, 173 police forces ticketed less than 50 persons per thousand of population, while 36 forces ticketed more than 250 persons per thousand. Figures from several pairs of cities of similar size will illustrate the differences involved. The police in Boston and Dallas, two

9. To secure these figures, in 1965 I sent letters to the chiefs of police of the 696 cities, towns, and townships in the United States with 1960 populations greater than 25,000. 508 (73 percent) returned information concerning 1964 ticketing and the size and organization of their forces. To check the possibility that the chiefs would overstate their ticket figures, responses from chiefs in one state (Massachusetts) were compared with the actual lists of traffic tickets submitted to the state agency charged with driver-license control. Of the 180 chiefs reporting (in this state, all municipalities larger than 5,000 were surveyed), almost no chief's statements varied by more than 1 percent or 2 percent from the official records; occasional *large* variations resulted from the inclusion of *parking* tickets with the moving-violation figures. In the national study, any figures that differed markedly from those from cities of similar size were verified through a second letter to the chief to see if parking tickets had been included.

Table 1.   Tickets per 1,000 Motor Vehicles, 1964

Range	N	%
0– 49	74	14.6%
50– 99	98	19.3
100–149	74	14.6
150–199	72	14.2
200–249	51	10.0
250–299	46	9.1
300–349	29	5.7
350–399	18	3.5
400–449	13	2.6
450 and over	27	5.3
Unknown[a]	6	1.2
	508	100.1%[b]
		$\overline{X} = 185$, $s = 144$

Sources. For Tables 1–3 information on the number of tickets and the number of policemen were obtained from each police department; information on the number of motor vehicles registered in each city was obtained from state motor vehicle departments or safety organizations; population figures are from the 1960 Census.

[a] Cities whose motor-vehicle registration figures were impossible to obtain.

[b] Total does not add to 100% because of rounding.

Table 2.   Tickets per 1,000 Population, 1964

Range	N	%
0– 49	173	34.1%
50– 99	127	25.0
100–149	83	16.3
150–199	61	12.0
200–249	28	5.5
250–299	19	3.7
300 and over	17	3.3
	508	99.9%[a]
		$\overline{X} = 104$, $s = 87$

[a] Total does not add to 100% because of rounding.

Table 3. Tickets per Policeman, 1964

Range	N	%
0– 24	125	24.6%
25– 49	114	22.4
50– 74	68	13.4
75– 99	65	12.8
100–124	64	12.6
125–149	23	4.5
150–174	25	4.9
175–199	11	2.2
200 and over	12	2.4
Unknown[a]	1	0.2
	508	100.0%

$$\overline{X} = 70, \quad s = 58$$

[a] A city for which it was impossible to learn the size of the police force.

cities that in 1960 had populations of approximately 700,000, wrote 11,242 and 273,626 moving-violation tickets respectively— a twenty-four-fold difference. Niagara Falls, New York, and Wichita Falls, Texas, with populations of slightly over 100,000 in 1960, saw 1,245 and 10,211 tickets in 1964. Police in Springfield, Massachusetts, wrote 14,720 tickets, while their counterparts in Grand Rapids, Michigan (also with a population of 175,000), were writing 36,727. Finally, in Cambridge and Somerville, Massachusetts, two adjacent cities with populations of 100,000, the police wrote 5,457 and 750 tickets respectively.

In the absence of data on the *actual* number of traffic violations committed in each city during 1964, these three sets of figures—tickets per thousand motor vehicles, tickets per thousand population, and tickets per policeman—were offered as gross measures of the effective rate of enforcement in these cities. It can easily be argued, however, that there is little relation between the ultimate data sought (actual violations) and the substitute bases used (motor vehicles, population, policemen): drivers in one city may be more law-abiding than those in another; traffic congestion, street layout, and weather conditions may make speeding more difficult in some cities than in others; some cities may rely more on the automobile rather than on mass transit as a means of transportation. Variations in state (and occasionally local) laws may make conduct illegal in one state and acceptable in another. The figure on tickets per thousand registered motor vehicles leaves out the movement of commuters entering or leaving the city in which they work, as well as that of tourists passing through; the tickets per thousand population also ignores any changes in population between 1960 and 1964.

Although each of these measures of the effective level of traffic-law enforcement is thus somewhat suspect, it is nevertheless hard to believe that the probable discrepancies between the number of actual violations and the bases used can explain *all* of the variation among the cities—the fact that the Dallas police ticketed 2,334 percent more motorists than the Boston police, the fact that the Cambridge police ticketed seven times as many motorists as the police in neighboring Somerville, or the fact that 173 police forces ticketed less than 50 persons per thousand population while 36 forces ticketed more than 250 persons per thousand. The gross validity, at least, of the three measures is supported by the high degree of correlation among them[10] and by my personal observation of enforcement policies in the police departments I visited (in thirty cities and towns in Massachusetts).

10. Pearsonian product-moment correlations between the three measures are:

	r
Tickets/1,000 motor vehicles—Tickets/1,000 population	.89
Tickets/1,000 motor vehicles—Tickets/Policeman	.82
Tickets/1,000 population—Tickets/Policeman	.85

Traffic-Law Enforcement in Massachusetts. To guard against the possibility that my nation-wide figures simply disguise variations in laws, driving habits, and local customs (and, therefore, indicate that police forces are responding similarly to varying rates of violation), we might look at the performance of police forces in one state, Massachusetts. Table 4 shows that, although

Table 4. Tickets per 1,000 Motor Vehicles in Massachusetts Cities Larger than 25,000 Population, 1964

Range	N	%
0– 49	32	66.7%
50– 99	10	20.8
100–149	3	6.3
150–199	2	4.2
200–249	1	2.1
	48	100.1%
		$\overline{X} = 47, \; s = 42$

Sources. 1960 population was obtained from the 1960 Census. The number of persons ticketed was ascertained from audit sheets of traffic-ticket books contained at the Registry of Motor Vehicles in Boston. The number of motor vehicles registered in a city or town in 1964 was obtained from the Massachusetts Department of Taxation.

the average effective level of enforcement is much lower, the range of variation within the state is almost as great as it is throughout the nation. Finally, Table 5 shows the variation among cities of over 50,000 people within the Boston metropolitan area.

If these figures, from Massachusetts and from throughout the United States, reflect significant variations among cities in the level of enforcement, we must ask how and why these variations arise. One possible explanation might be that the variations are produced by differences in the recruitment, values, and training

Table 5. Persons Ticketed in Larger Cities in the Boston Area, 1964

City	1960 Population	Persons ticketed	Persons ticketed per 1,000 motor vehicles
Waltham	55,413	4,901	158
Cambridge	107,716	5,457	143
Brookline	54,004	3,550	128
Boston	697,197	11,242	54
Brockton	72,813	2,200	52
Newton	92,384	2,575	49
Lowell	92,107	1,412	37
Quincy	87,409	1,318	30
Medford	64,971	782	27
Lawrence	70,933	705	23
Somerville	94,697	750	21
Malden	57,676	416	17
Lynn	94,478	502	12

of individual policemen. We all know or have heard of nice traffic officers who could be talked out of tickets and of tough officers who could not. Although such variations among individual policemen certainly exist, I doubt that we can give them a place of prime importance in explaining the great intercity variations. Since every police department contains men of varying interests and abilities, *any* police chief can find or train nice or tough traffic men if he wants to. Furthermore, at least in the police departments to be analyzed in this book, the effective rates of enforcement seem to be more influenced by departmental values than by individuals' attitudes: some men in Waltham or Cambridge who individually wrote more traffic tickets in a year than the entire police forces of Lynn or Malden seemed to be personally *less* interested in traffic work than some policemen in the latter cities.

If variations in the attitudes of individual officers are inadequate explanations for the intercity variations I have noted, what alternatives are left? Two hypotheses will be explored in this volume. The first is that the effective level of traffic-law enforcement in a community is the product of the interests, attitudes, and activities of the local police chief or officer setting enforcement policy in each police department; his preferences will be reflected in the allocation of men, time, and other resources among the various functions assigned to the department. The second hypothesis is that these official preferences, and the enforcement rates stemming from them, are moderately correlated with some characteristics of the communities in which the police departments operate, most notably with the degree of geographic stability rather than mobility of the city's population.

The chapters to follow explore these questions on several different levels. Part One looks at traffic-law enforcement in one state, Massachusetts. Following a description of the entire system of enforcement in the state, including an appraisal of the relative importance of the police, the courts, and the Registry of Motor Vehicles, four case studies illustrate different departments' approaches to their traffic-enforcement functions. Part Two, broader in focus, examines the nature and extent of public pressures on the police, the relation between community characteristics and police traffic policies, and internal organizational constraints on police policy formation.

It should also be made clear at this point what this book does *not* purport to study. First, it concerns the enforcement of *moving*-traffic laws, not parking regulations. Second, I am concerned with the policies of police departments, not of individual policemen. Third, I look only at general-purpose local police departments, even though other agencies play a role in the enforcement of a state's traffic laws; since traffic duties are viewed as being in competition with other police responsibilities (homicide, burglary, prostitution, and so on) for limited police resources, only multifunctional local agencies will be studied. Finally, this study looks at police forces at only one point in time (1964-65). For ease of presentation, the case studies are written in the present tense, even though subsequent changes in laws and personnel make some of the conclusions inaccurate characterizations of policies in effect in those cities today.[11]

The Four Cities. The four cities and police departments to be described in Part One were chosen solely on the basis of their traffic policies. The first, Lynn, had the lowest rate of ticket writing of any city with a population over 50,000 in the Boston area; Waltham had the highest rate of enforcement in this group of cities. The third city, Malden, had the second lowest rate of enforcement, and also illustrates how men designated as enforcement specialists will act in a city that places greater emphasis upon courtesy and restraint than upon vigorous enforcement. Finally, Cambridge, the second most active enforcer of traffic laws in the Boston area, shows how a new chief, interested in traffic work, redirects the policies of his men to increase the number of tickets written.

Although effective rates of enforcement, rather than social, economic, or political factors, were the bases used to select the four cities, some background data might be introduced at this point, both to describe the cities and to permit the reader to see them in relation to other cities in the United States. Geographi-

11. Waltham's Chief Carmody, for example, retired in 1966 and was replaced by a man who orders intensive traffic enforcement only in response to specific citizen complaints. Cambridge's Chief Brennan died in 1967.

cally, all four cities are part of the Boston metropolitan area, distributed along a line about fifteen miles long just to the north of the core city. A portion of each city's labor force works in Boston, but each also has a substantial industrial base of its own, and both Cambridge and Waltham also profit from educational institutions (two colleges and Harvard University and Massachusetts Institute of Technology in Cambridge; Brandeis University in Waltham).

As the 1960 Census data in Table 6 illustrate, Lynn, Waltham, and Malden have fairly similar demographic and housing characteristics, with Waltham somewhat more prosperous and Lynn somewhat less so than the others. All employ some variety of the Plan B—weak mayor, strong council—form of government. In many respects, Cambridge is unlike the other cities. It is the last major city in the United States to use the proportional-representation system of voting in conjunction with the council-manager form of government. As will be illustrated in Chapter Five, Cambridge is divided into two strikingly different (and antagonistic) population groups—a professional and managerial class clustered around Harvard, and a large working-class population spread through North and East Cambridge. Comparative census data illustrate this division: Cambridge has a higher proportion of low-income families (15 percent) than any of the other three cities except Lynn; yet it also has a higher proportion of upper-income families (17 percent) than any of the other cities except Waltham.

Looking at the political life of the four cities, we note that they are all strongly Democratic in state and national politics, giving about 65 percent of their votes to Kennedy in 1960 and 75 percent to Johnson in 1964. In nonpartisan local affairs, however, strong differences appear. Using the typology of roles of local

N.B.

Table 6. Police, Demographic, and Housing Characteristics for Four Cities

Category	Lynn	Waltham	Malden	Cambridge	Boston metropolitan area
Persons ticketed, 1964	502	4,901	416	5,407	
Tickets per 1,000 motor vehicles, 1964	11.9	158.3	16.8	143.0	
Total police	184	100	120	230	
Police per 1,000 population	1.99	1.72	2.10	2.21	
Population, 1960	94,478	55,413	57,676	107,716	2,589,301
Population change, 1930–1960	–8%	41%	–.6%	–5%	19%
Foreign stock	43%	44%	47%	44%	42%
Non-white	1.6%	0.4%	1.3%	6.3%	3.4%
In white-collar occupations[a]	39%	41%	45%	51%	50%
Median years of schooling	11.0	11.6	11.1	12.0	12.1
Median family income	$6,021	$6,804	$6,194	$5,923	$6,687
Family income under $3,000	15%	8%	12%	15%	11%
Family income over $10,000	14%	20%	13%	17%	21%
Dwelling units owner-occupied	44%	55%	48%	23%	52%
Dwelling units in sound condition	86%	93%	87%	86%	84%
Median gross rent (per month)	$78	$92	$83	$79	$82
Per capita general expenditures (excluding education), 1960	$139	$126	$144	$160	
Form of government	mayor-council	mayor-council	mayor-council	council-manager	

Source. 1960 Census of Population and 1960 Census of Housing.

[a] White-collar occupations: professional, managerial, clerical, and sales occupations according to Census classifications.

government developed by Williams and Adrian,[12] we see that Lynn and Malden are dominated by an ethos of caretaker government—maintaining traditional services and keeping tax rates down. Waltham, on the other hand, displays in limited form what Williams and Adrian characterize as a government seeking to promote economic growth, expanding the population and wealth of the community.

Table 7. Dominant Roles of Local Government in Four Cities

Role	Low		Medium	High
Economic growth	Lynn	Malden	Cambridge, A	Waltham
Life's amenities	Lynn Malden	Waltham	Cambridge, A	
Caretaker	Waltham		Cambridge, B	Lynn Malden
Arbiter	Lynn Malden Waltham			Cambridge, C

Note. For the reasons described in the text, each faction in Cambridge is listed separately: A, upper middle class; B, working class; C, mediating group.

In politics as in demography, it is difficult to classify Cambridge. The working-class segment of Cambridge endorses the caretaker role preferred in Lynn and Malden. The upper-middle-class population in Cambridge supports economic growth and what Williams and Adrian call "providing and securing life's amenities"; local government, according to these residents, should provide for the consumer rather than the producer needs of its

12. Oliver P. Williams, "A Typology for Comparative Local Government," *Midwest Journal of Political Science,* II (May 1961), 150–164; and Oliver P. Williams and Charles R. Adrian, *Four Cities: A Study in Comparative Policy-Making* (Philadelphia: University of Pennsylvania Press, 1963).

citizens. Safety, beauty, and convenience are their concerns. Finally, as we shall see, a third group in Cambridge political life has been able in recent years to hold office by playing the role of "arbitrating among conflicting interests," mediating the recurrent hostilities between Cambridge's working and professional classes.

While none of the four cities to be studied in this book represents a "pure" type, I shall conclude this introductory chapter by ranking them in terms of the four Williams and Adrian categories (Table 7).

After describing formal arrangements for traffic-law enforcement in Massachusetts, we shall look at these four cities and then at the factors influencing enforcement policies throughout the United States.

Part I / Traffic-Law Enforcement in Massachusetts

1 / The Formal Organization

To understand the context in which police decisionmaking in the area of traffic-law enforcement takes place, we should begin by isolating the area of discretion controlled by the police, rather than by other agencies, and by identifying formal constraints that influence the operation of police departments. First, we will look at Massachusetts police actions regarding traffic vis-à-vis the role of courts and the Massachusetts Registry of Motor Vehicles. Second, we will look at the distribution of formal authority within Massachusetts local police departments, particularly at the extent to which the operations of the department are controlled by the police chief and higher officers rather than by state statutes and local ordinances.

Distribution of Authority between Enforcement Institutions. Like the American federal system, the system of traffic regulation in Massachusetts is divided both territorially and procedurally.[1] Massachusetts, like the other New England states, is divided into counties, cities, and towns. But unlike many states, Massachusetts assigns no traffic-control functions to its counties and county sheriffs.[2] The territorial division of the traffic-regulation system, then, is among the legislature, the courts, and the

1. See the analysis of American federalism in Arthur Maass, ed., *Area and Power* (Glencoe: Free Press, 1959).

2. For a detailed statement of the powers of Massachusetts sheriffs, see Massachusetts Legislative Research Council, *Report Relative to County Government in Massachusetts,* House Report No. 3131 (1963).

Registry of Motor Vehicles, acting at the state level, and the police forces that act in specific local areas. (The state police and the Metropolitan District Police, although creatures of the state, can be assigned to this latter category: the state police mainly enforce traffic laws on the rural state highways, and the Metropolitan District Police act only on Metropolitan District Commission highways around Boston.) Procedurally, the system of traffic regulation is divided among lawmaking, law enforcing, and adjudicating and punishing agencies.

The process of lawmaking is divided between the state legislature and the municipalities. The legislature passes state-wide laws regulating traffic, such as that no one may drive without a license, that all motor vehicles must be registered, and that certain types of conduct—speeding, driving while under the influence of alcohol, failure to have adequate equipment—are forbidden and will lead to certain penalties. The legislature also determines, within the limits of the state and federal constitutions, the procedures by which traffic regulations are enacted by municipal legislative bodies—the city council or the annual town meeting. The municipalities can, for example, pass ordinances regarding parking, speed limits, stop signs, and one-way streets. With the exception of parking ordinances, locally enacted traffic regulations must be approved by state agencies: the Registry of Motor Vehicles must approve all speed limits; the Department of Public Works must approve other restrictions upon traffic movement such as stop signs, traffic lights, and one-way signs. Fines resulting from violations of local ordinances go to the municipalities; fines from violations of state traffic laws go to the counties in which the violations occur.[3]

3. Massachusetts General Laws Chapter 85, paragraphs 2, 10; Chapter 280, paragraph 2; Chapter 90, paragraphs 18, 20A. Abbreviated hereafter.

The process of traffic-law enforcement is shared by a number of agencies, but there is a fairly sharp territorial division of labor. In addition to the city and town police forces, Massachusetts traffic laws are enforced by the state police, the Metropolitan District Police, and the Registry of Motor Vehicles. The uniformed division of the state police contains about 490 men, distributed across the state. Although the state troopers have police powers throughout the state, they generally confine their traffic-enforcement activities to state highways outside the metropolitan areas. The Metropolitan District Police (a division of the Metropolitan District Commission, which provides highways, parks, water, and sewage disposal for certain cities and towns in the Boston area) patrol 185 miles of MDC-maintained highways. The Registry of Motor Vehicles is the only agency enforcing traffic laws beyond a restricted area; in addition to its regular license-suspending activities, a number of its employees (eight on a full-time basis, others from time to time) conduct "selective enforcement" operations throughout the state, in both rural and urban areas.

In Massachusetts, the process of adjudication of and punishment for violations of traffic laws is divided between the courts and the Registry of Motor Vehicles. The courts, using normal judicial procedures, impose fines and jail sentences on traffic violators; the Registry, using administrative procedures, suspends or revokes driving privileges. The basic units of the Massachusetts court system are the seventy-three district courts.[4] A court district may vary in size from a part of the city of Boston to most

4. For a more detailed description of the Massachusetts court system, see Edwin A. Powers, *The Basic Structure of the Administration of Criminal Justice in Massachusetts* (4th ed., Boston: Massachusetts Department of Correction, 1964), pp. 22–29.

of a rural county in the western part of the state. All justices are appointed for life by the governor, with the consent of the executive council. Although they are appointed to sit in a particular court, they need not be residents of that court district and may be assigned by the chief justice of the district courts to sit in other districts. Justices in the fifty largest district courts receive $20,000 per year and serve on a full-time basis. Each district court also has at least one "special justice," who serves part-time and is paid on a *per diem* basis.

All criminal cases begin in the district courts, but they may wind up in the county-wide superior courts. The district courts lack jurisdiction over felonies punishable by a prison sentence of more than five years; defendants arraigned in the district courts on one of these charges will be bound over for the superior court. Further, a person convicted in the district court can appeal to the superior court and receive a trial *de novo*, either with or without a jury.[5] In all but two courts, there are no juries in the district courts; a defendant who wishes a jury trial must appeal his conviction to the superior court.

The task of prosecuting criminal cases is divided between the district attorneys, elected on a county-wide partisan ballot, and the police prosecutors, appointed by individual police chiefs. All criminal work in the district courts is handled by the prosecutors, who almost never have formal legal training. The district attorneys, who must be lawyers, only prosecute cases that have been brought into the superior courts.

The Massachusetts Registry of Motor Vehicles has several functions related to traffic-law enforcement. The basic one is the issuance of driving licenses and motor-vehicle registration certificates. Since 1962, it has also been required to prepare, issue, and

5. Mass. G.L. Ch. 218 §30.

audit the books of tickets in which traffic violations are recorded (these tickets will be discussed shortly). The Registry's most significant role in the sphere of traffic-law enforcement involves suspending or revoking driving privileges.

Procedures Used in Handling Traffic Violations. To see how these basic units function in Massachusetts, we might trace the handling of a normal moving violation—that is, one neither so trivial that the motorist escapes with a verbal warning nor so serious that the motorist is immediately arrested.

The basic mechanism used in traffic-law enforcement is the traffic ticket. Until 1962, traffic tickets were distributed and controlled by the district courts; court clerks were required to send to the Registry abstracts of all motor-vehicle cases. Since 1962, traffic tickets have been printed, numbered, and issued in quintuplicate by the Registry of Motor Vehicles. Books of tickets are assigned to local police chiefs, who must account to the Registry for the use made of each book and each ticket. The 1962 law provided that "any police officer assigned to traffic enforcement duty" is supposed to be given one of these books, and to fill out and give to violators a Registry ticket at the scene of the violation "whenever possible."[6] In 1964, only the state police and local police forces in 28 of 180 cities and towns issued Registry ticket books to some or all of their officers.[7] The other police forces kept their Registry books at headquarters, and officers recorded necessary information in notebooks or on forms provided by their department. The Registry forms were filled out at headquarters

6. Mass. G.L. Ch. 90 §27; Ch. 90C §2.
7. This information was gathered from interviews with police chiefs in January 1965 and from studies of the ticket-book audit sheets collected at the Registry of Motor Vehicles.

only if official action (a formal warning, prosecution in court, or suspension by the Registry) was ought. The traffic tickets used in Massachusetts while I was conducting this study differed in at least three ways from the "Uniform Traffic Ticket and Complaint" endorsed by the American Bar Association, which is used in one or more communities in 43 states.[8] First, the uniform tickets are given to the motorist on the spot, unless he evades apprehension. In most cities and towns in Massachusetts, as mentioned earlier, the official Registry ticket was mailed to the motorist from police headquarters. Second, the uniform ticket is in and of itself an order to appear in court; as the late chief justice of the New Jersey Supreme Court, Arthur T. Vanderbilt, said, "This kind of ticket canot be killed without the active aid of three public officials—the court, police headquarters, and the individual officer."[9] The Massachusetts ticket was used to give a written warning or to ask for Registry action as well as to initiate court action; the district courts only controlled those violations on which the police decided to seek court action.

Under the uniform-ticket system, the arresting officer decides whether the motorist will be brought into court or simply be given a verbal warning. In Massachusetts, even in those cities where policemen carried the Registry books, the decision was not made by them. Although the arresting officer could, depending upon department custom, *suggest* the recommendation to be made on a ticket, the final recommendation was written on the ticket by "the police chief or an officer of a rank not lower than sergeant."[10] The theoretical purpose of this arrangement, according to many

8. See American Bar Association Traffic Court Program, *Uniform Traffic Ticket and Complaint* (Lansing, Mich.: Weger Governmental Systems, 1958).

9. *Ibid.*, p. 20.

10. Mass. G.L. Ch. 90C §2.

of the police chiefs I interviewed, was to see to it that all recommendations were based upon uniform standards and that individual officers did not conduct vendettas against personal enemies. The actual effect of this arrangement, as will be seen throughout this book, was to centralize ticket fixing, as well as recommendations, in the hands of the police chief or his senior officers. (The operation of the system of ticket fixing will be discussed in Chapter Six.)

Once a Registry ticket was written, Massachusetts police chiefs could make one of four recommendations. They might mark it "Warning" or "Registry action," and the Registry would decide whether suspension was merited. They might mark it for court action and seek a complaint against the motorist. Finally, they might void a ticket, giving the Registry "a full explanation for this action."[11] Lest this be thought an onerous restriction, it might be mentioned that most explanations in the Registry files say simply "ticket lost," "citation mutilated," or "duplicate of above ticket"; no one in the Registry had the time or inclination to demand more complete explanations from police chiefs. The chiefs, however, seem to think that someone at the Registry notices voided tickets, so ticket fixing seldom takes the form of voiding a Registry ticket. As will be seen later, most fixing involves marking a Registry ticket warning, if a *departmental* ticket form was not simply destroyed.

The procedure used in handling traffic violations in court changed as my study was underway. Until 1965, traffic cases were processed like other criminal matters, and violators had to appear in court no matter whether they wished to plead guilty or not guilty. Starting in January 1, 1965, most traffic violators who wish to plead guilty can simply sign a waiver of trial and mail to the

11. *Ibid.*

court clerk a fine based upon a uniform state-wide schedule of fines established by the chief justice of the district courts. The "pay by mail" system does not apply to offenses carrying possible prison sentences or fines of more than $50 or to parking violations (local ordinances usually permit paying parking fines by mail); juvenile offenders and persons who have been convicted of moving violations within the past twelve months are also barred from paying fines by mail.

One final aspect of the processing of traffic violations might be mentioned at this point, to avoid confusion later. This concerns the appearance of police officers as witnesses. A number of district courts require the officer who writes a traffic ticket to be in court when the motorist is ordered to appear. Other courts simply wait to see if the motorist will plead not guilty; if he does, the officer is called into court or a future trial date is set. The rule in effect will be specified for each city studied. (The impact of this court-appearance requirement will be analyzed in Chapter Seven.)

Discretion in the Administration of Traffic Laws. Each of several agencies has available to it a range of choices regarding the manner in which traffic laws will be administered. The police can decide whether to stop an observed violator, whether to write a ticket, and whether to send a ticketed violator to court. Judges can decide whether to convict a motorist and what penalties to impose upon convicted defendants. The Registry of Motor Vehicles can choose from a wide range of sanctions in handling convicted or unconvicted motorists. To understand the relative roles of each of these agencies in traffic-law enforcement, we should look more closely at the decisions made by each.

Since, as noted in the introduction, it is impossible to ascertain how many violations of traffic laws actually take place in each city, there are no hard data on the percentage of violators who are stopped by police, or on the percentage of those stopped who are given a ticket rather than a verbal warning. We can, however, determine whether policemen, having written a ticket, decide to bring motorists into court. Table 8 shows the variations among

Table 8. Massachusetts Police-Department Ticket Recommendations

% to court	Number of departments	%
0– 19	19	10.6
20– 39	30	16.7
40– 59	48	26.7
60– 79	34	18.9
80–100	42	23.3
Unknown	7	3.9
	180	100.1
		$\overline{X} = 48.9, \ s = 30.9$

Source. These figures were calculated from ticket-book audit sheets filed with the Registry of Motor Vehicles in Boston. When the number of traffic tickets written by a police force in 1964 exceeded 500, a sample (every second sheet, every third sheet, etc.) was used so that at least 500 tickets would be studied. The "unknown" figures represent police forces that failed to file audit sheets at the Registry. The "court" figures include persons who were arrested at the scene of the violation.

the 180 Massachusetts police departments (in cities and towns of over 5,000) in the percentage of tickets written by each department which were marked for court action rather than for warnings or Registry action. In other words, even though each of these tickets was presumably based upon evidence of a violation serious enough to be noted on the motorist's record, the percentage of these tickets which led to court action varied widely: motorists in 42 jurisdictions faced an 80 percent chance of being summoned into court if ticketed; motorists in 19 cities and towns stood less than a 20 percent chance of being so inconvenienced. To cite two examples, the Brookline police ticketed 3,550 persons in 1964 and brought 4 percent of them to court; the Waltham police ticketed 4,901 persons and brought 82.5 percent of them to court.

These figures show a broad variation in the use of the police departments' discretionary power. What happens to motorists who are brought to court? In 1963, the Massachusetts district courts handled 178,000 traffic cases: 7.7 percent were dismissed before trial; 7.2 percent of the defendants pleaded not guilty, and 81.2 percent of those who pleaded not guilty were convicted. In

Table 9.   Massachusetts District-Court Actions in Traffic Cases, 1963

% acquitted	Number of courts	%
0– 4	64	87.6
5– 9	7	9.6
10–14	1	1.4
15–19	1	1.4
	73	100.0
		$\overline{X} = 2.7, \; s = 2.9$

general, the defendants in 98.6 percent of all traffic cases were convicted in the district courts in 1963. The variations among the 73 courts in the percentage of traffic defendants acquitted is shown in Table 9.

Putting these police and court figures together, we can see that for all intents and purposes the police decision to ticket and send a motorist to court is the critical point in the enforcement process—once a ticket is marked for court action, a motorist is almost certain to be convicted whether he pleads guilty or not guilty. Even in the most serious traffic offenses—driving while intoxicated and driving so as to endanger the public—the district courts convicted almost as many defendants (88 percent and 86 percent) as in the minor cases, although much higher proportions (55 percent and 52 percent) had pleaded not guilty.

Apart from the activities of the courts, the Registry of Motor Vehicles has played an important role in controlling traffic violators. The area of discretion open to the Registry has varied to some extent over the years. From 1953 to 1960, license suspension in Massachusetts was governed by a point system—conviction of a traffic offense meant that a fixed number of points would be charged against an operator's record; his license was automatically suspended when a stated number of points had been accumulated.[12] Since 1960, license suspension has been governed by a combination of specific rules and a general grant of discretionary power to the Registrar. As in other types of administrative proceedings, the Registrar must give a motorist adequate notice and the opportunity for a hearing; an aggrieved person may appeal the Registrar's decision to a Board of Appeal on Motor Vehicle Liability Policies and Bonds and then to the superior courts.[13]

The basic grant of power to the Registrar of Motor Vehicles is almost unlimited:

> The registrar may suspend or revoke any certificate of registration or any license issued under this chapter, after due hearing, *for any cause which he may deem sufficient,* and may suspend the license of any operator . . . *whenever he has reason to believe that the holder thereof is an improper or incompetent person to operate motor vehicles, or is operating improperly or so as to endanger the public;* and neither the certificate of registration nor the license shall be

12. Mass. G.L. Ch. 90A, added by Stat. 1953, Ch. 570; repealed by Stat. 1960, Ch. 390.
13. Mass. G.L. Ch. 90 §§22, 28; Ch. 30A §14.

reissued unless, upon examination or investigation, or after a hearing, the registrar determines that the operator should again be permitted to operate.[14]

In addition to this general grant of discretionary power, the legislature has also required suspension for specified lengths of time for failing to answer a summons for a parking violation, committing three moving violations within a year, failing to satisfy a judgment in an accident case, driving under the influence of alcohol or drugs, leaving the scene of an accident, using a motor vehicle without authority (joyriding), or failing to register an automobile or to have adequate insurance coverage.[15] The Registrar is also required to suspend licenses, but for lengths of time that are at his discretion, when the operator is charged with "driving negligently so as to endanger the lives or safety of the public," failing to report an accident, or failing to have adequate equipment.[16]

The Registrar's license-suspending powers are both narrower and wider than these statutes might suggest. In 1952, the Massachusetts Supreme Judicial Court ruled that if the Registrar bases a suspension on a specific grant of power (in this case, the duty to suspend for driving under the influence of alcohol), he must prove that the operator had in fact violated that statute. (Here the Registrar proved that the motorist had been driving after drinking, but not that he was "operating under the influence."[17]) This decision left untouched the Registrar's general power to suspend the licenses of "improper or incompetent op-

14. Mass. G.L. Ch. 90 §22. Italics added.
15. Mass. G.L. Ch. 90 §§20, 20A, 22A, 24, 29, 34H.
16. Mass. G.L. Ch. 90 §§2, 24, 26.
17. *Wall v. Registrar of Motor Vehicles*, 329 Mass. 20, 106 N.E.2d 428 (1952).

erators." As in other administrative proceedings, the courts may also overturn a ruling by a Registrar if it is "unwarranted by facts," "arbitrary or capricious," and so on.[18]

The Registrar's powers have been expanded in three directions. First, in 1954, the United States Court of Appeals for the First Circuit ruled that, whereas operating an automobile is a "liberty" subject to the protection of the Fourteenth Amendment, the procedures provided in Massachusetts for suspending licenses (notice, hearing, appeal) satisfied the requirement of due process— so there are almost no *constitutional* limits on the Registrar's powers.[19] Second, the state attorney general ruled in 1925 that the Registrar's discretion "is not limited merely to a consideration of the violation of motor vehicle laws or of the right of the public to use public ways in safety," approving a suspension when the motorist used his car to commit a felony.[20] Some registrars have used this discretionary power to harass juveniles, although one recent registrar announced that he would refuse "to revoke or suspend the licenses of youths involved in 'rumbles' or clashes with the law unless they are directly related to improper motor vehicle operation."[21] Finally, it must be noted that the Registrar's power does not depend upon a conviction on a motor-vehicle violation. First, the police may simply notify the Registry that Driver X was apprehended while doing such-and-such, and the Registrar can act without any court action. Second, the Registrar can and does suspend licenses even when the operator has been acquitted in court, arguing that the standards to be applied in determining whether X is an "improper or incompetent operator" are not

18. Mass. G.L. Ch. 30A §14(8).

19. *Wall v. King,* 206 F. 2d 878 (1953), *cert. den.,* 346 U.S. 915 (1954).

20. Opinions of the Massachusetts Attorney General, VII (1925), 611.

21. Thomas C. Gallagher, "Registrar on the Way Out?" *Boston Herald,* January 14, 1965.

necessarily those to be used by a judge in deciding whether X has violated the law.[22]

Although I am not attempting to offer a complete appraisal of the Registry's role in traffic-law enforcement, two comments about the Registry's operations should be made, in order to qualify the picture painted by this description of its legal powers. The first is that, simply for lack of manpower, the Registry has never been able to process all of the information submitted to it. In 1963, for example, it received 255,000 accident reports and 33,000 notices from insurance companies that compulsory liability policies had been canceled.[23]

In 1965, the Registry automated all of its enforcement bookkeeping—all violation notices are now fed into a computer that separates out those violators whose past records (say, two previous moving violations within a year) might suggest suspension. The decision to suspend, however, is made by human examiners.[24] At the time my study was made (1964), the system used was roughly this: hearings officers scanned all violation notices received by the Registry. Offenses deemed "serious" were studied for possible suspension, regardless of the recommendations made on the ticket by local police. When a violation was deemed minor but had been sent to court by the police, the Registry mailed the motorist a letter warning him against future violations. Minor violations that had not been sent to court (where the police marked a ticket "Warning" or "Registry") were simply dropped

22. For several years, unsuccessful attempts have been made in the legislature to preclude suspension when an operator has been acquitted in court. See, e.g., Massachusetts Legislature, Senate Bill No. 154 (1964).

23. Massachusetts Registry of Motor Vehicles, *Summary of 1963 Enforcement Activities* (1964).

24. Stanley Eams, " 'Big Brother' Eyes Licenses," *Boston Herald,* October 7, 1964.

into the motorist's file, and no attempt was made to see if the motorist had accumulated violation slips in the past.[25] The computerized process is designed to guarantee that *all* violation notices are compared with the past record of the motorist.

It is difficult to estimate the effect of the pre-computer system upon Registry suspension activities. Of the 255,000 violation notices received by the Registry in 1963, 144,000 were taken to court. The Registry suspended, for varying lengths of time, 56,000 licenses (46,000 additional licenses or registrations were suspended because of insurance cancellations or failure to register a motor vehicle, answer a parking summons, or satisfy a property-damage judgment).[26] The Registrar estimated in 1964 that the automated process would uncover 200,000 more suspension cases per year than the manual filing system.[27] It was also disclosed in 1965 that the Registry had been unable to process over 30,000 cases in which a motorist had failed to answer a parking-violation summons—an offense supposedly meriting automatic suspension.[28]

The second aspect of Registry operations which affects its license-suspending activities has been variously described as "politics," "favoritism," or "corruption." During a three-year investigation of crime and corruption throughout the state, the Massachusetts Crime Commission

found evidence of improper action and political preference

25. Interview with Deputy Registrar of Motor Vehicles John F. Adams, October 1, 1964. The power of the courts to recommend suspension "in such cases as they may deem necessary" is found in Mass. G.L. Ch. 90 §27.

26. Registry of Motor Vehicles, *Summary of 1963 Enforcement Activities.*

27. Eams, "'Big Brother' Eyes Licenses."

28. Robert F. Hannan, "30,000 Parking Tag Backlog Disclosed," *Boston Herald,* April 17, 1965.

in past years in connection with suspensions and revocations of licenses and in connection with violations of the laws relating to overweight trucks . . . The Commission is of the opinion that [the power to suspend licenses] has not been exercised impartially in the past and that the present system invites corruption.[29]

This appraisal of earlier conditions in the Registry was affirmed by a number of the police chiefs I interviewed. Each told of motorists who were apprehended for violations meriting suspension who avoided or minimized license suspension by contacting a legislator or other political figure.

Registry corruption or favoritism can take one of two forms. The first is ludicrously simple—since violations, until the computerized filing system was put into operation, were recorded only on the violation slips placed in individual files, all evidence could be destroyed if a corrupt file clerk were to rifle the files; security procedures were almost nonexistent.

The second phase of Registry activity that can lead to attempts to use political influence is that of discretionary suspensions. As mentioned earlier, many of the statutory bases for suspension (such as improper or incompetent operation) are quite broad, and there are no time periods set by statute for suspension in these and some other cases (such as driving to endanger). Registrars have given their examiners certain guidelines on grounds for and length of suspension in these cases, but the examiners are also directed to consider the "habits and character" of the motorist. Given this flexibility, politicians are practically invited to intercede for constituents. After calling for a reorganization of the

29. Massachusetts Crime Commission, *Comprehensive Report*, I (1965), 42–43.

Registry, a major recommendation of the Massachusetts Crime Commission was that the Registry's rules and regulations should "contain a table of violations for which drivers' licenses and registrations of motor vehicles will be suspended or revoked. The table shall contain stated periods of suspension applicable to such violations. To the extent that periods of suspension are not provided by statute, they shall be fixed by the rules and regulations."[30] (Lest it be thought that these flexible standards always work in favor of motorists, it should also be mentioned that police chiefs frequently call the Registry to ask that discretionary suspensions be continued beyond the minimum period suggested by the Registrar's guidelines. Sharing with the Registry a suspicion of judges and juries, the chiefs also actively defend the Registrar's power to suspend even when the motorist has been acquitted in court.)

The Organization of Local Police Departments. To a large extent, the organization of Massachusetts police departments is controlled by a combination of state statutes and local ordinances. As in many other states, the Massachusetts legislature (the General Court) retains authority over the operation of all municipalities. The state constitution, for example, provides that

> the general court shall have full power and authority to erect and constitute municipal or city governments in any corporate town or towns in this commonwealth, and to grant to the inhabitants thereof such powers, privileges, and immunities, not repugnant to the constitution, as the general court may deem necessary or expedient for the regulation and government thereof . . . All by-laws made by such municipal or

30. *Ibid.*, II, E 38–39.

city government shall be subject, at all times, to be annulled by the general court.[31]

In line with "Dillon's rule," Massachusetts cities and towns have only those powers expressly or implicitly conferred upon them by the legislature.[32]

In several respects, Massachusetts cities and towns have more autonomy than these legal provisions might suggest. First, special legislative acts, applicable to only one city or town, are frequently permissive rather than mandatory. In 1962, for example, the legislature passed a bill creating a detective bureau in the Cambridge Police Department "subject to acceptance during the current year by the City of Cambridge."[33] Second, the legislature has allowed local voters to choose certain standardized forms of government. City voters, outside of Boston, can choose one of six forms of government—Plan A (strong mayor, weak council), Plan B (weak mayor, strong council), Plan C (commission), Plan D (city manager), Plan E (city manager and a council elected by proportional representation), and Plan F (strong mayor, weak council, both chosen in partisan elections).[34] Of the cities studied in the following chapters, as I have said, Cambridge

31. Massachusetts Constitution, Article of Amendment II. In 1965, the legislature passed a constitutional amendment granting to cities and towns the power to amend their own charters and to adopt any ordinances not inconsistent with state laws or the constitution. Massachusetts Legislature, House Bill No. 461 (1965). The amendment was approved by the voters in a 1966 referendum. See also Massachusetts Legislative Research Council, *Report Relative to Municipal Home Rule,* Senate Report No. 580 (1961).

32. See John F. Dillon, *Commentaries on the Law of Municipal Corporations,* 5th ed. (Boston: Little, Brown, 1911), I, 448; and *Attorney General v. City of Lowell,* 246 Mass. 312 (1923).

33. Massachusetts Legislature, *Acts of 1962,* Ch. 668.

34. Mass. G.L. Ch. 43.

has a Plan E form of government; the others use some form of Plan B (weak mayor, strong council).

Regardless of the form of local government, state statutes play a large role in the organization and operation of local police forces. All cities in Massachusetts must give civil-service protection to their policemen, although they are free to choose whether or not to put their police chief under civil service;[35] in 1964, thirty-four of thirty-nine city police chiefs (including all four chiefs studied here) were under civil service. When local police departments are under the civil-service system, all examinations, appointments, promotions, and dismissals are administered by the state Division of Civil Service.[36] The major civil-service provisions affecting the organization of police departments are:

(1) Written competitive examinations for civil-service positions are held on a local basis—there are no state-wide lists of persons eligible for, say, the position of patrolman. All police examinations for similar positions are similar, however, and are based on a civil-service manual of instruction for applicants for police positions.[37]

(2) To be eligible for police entrance examinations, an applicant must: (a) be a citizen of the United States and have been a resident of the city or town for at least six months; (b) be between the ages of twenty-two and thirty-five; (c) not have been convicted of a felony (the state director may waive the rule af-

35. Mass. G.L. Ch. 31 §48.

36. See George C. S. Benson, *The Administration of the Civil Service in Massachusetts* (Cambridge: Harvard University Press, 1935); and League of Women Voters of Massachusetts, *Introduction to Civil Service Practices in Massachusetts* (Boston, 1959).

37. Massachusetts Division of Civil Service, *A Manual for the Instruction of Applicants for Examinations for the Police Services* (1964).

fecting persons who are "habitual users of intoxicating liquor" or who have been convicted of a crime if the penalty imposed was a fine of less than $100 or a jail sentence of less than six months); (d) "No rule or regulation shall be made setting up educational requirements as a condition for taking a civil service examination" except where expressly provided.[38] (No educational requirements have been set for any police position, and recent attempts to repeal this provision have been rejected by the legislature.)[39]

(3) Promotions are based entirely upon competitive examinations; there is no performance-rating system in the law. There must be at least four applicants for each examination; eligibility for promotional examinations is limited to persons in the next lower rank, unless eligibility is extended to find four applicants. In cities and towns of under 50,000, applicants for promotion must have been employed by the department for at least one year; in larger cities and towns, applicants must have been employed in the lowest rank (patrolman) for at least three years and in each higher rank for at least one year.[40]

(4) Persons receiving a passing grade of 70 percent are placed on a list in the following order: disabled veterans in order of grade, veterans in order of grade, and nonveterans in order of grade. The system thus provides "absolute" veterans' preference rather than simple bonus points for veterans. Veterans' preference applies to promotional as well as entrance examinations, and disabled veterans have preference in determining the order of

38. Massachusetts Division of Civil Service, *Civil Service Rules* (1946), Rule 4; Mass. G.L. Ch. 31, §§6A, 17, 48, 96A.

39. See, e.g., Massachusetts Legislature, House Bill No. 610 (1963).

40. See Massachusetts Legislative Research Council, *Report Relative to Civil Service Performance Rating,* House Report No. 2655 (1959); Mass. G.L. Ch. 31 §48.

layoff and re-employment.[41] (Since applicants for police positions must pass a quite strenuous physical test as well as a written examination, few disabled persons, veterans or otherwise, are accepted for police work. A person called to military duty *after* joining a police force could, however, become disabled and thus merit preference even though no longer able to pass the physical test.)

(5) All examination grades can be appealed to the director of civil service, then to the Civil Service Commission, and finally to the district courts.[42] In 1962, 34,885 persons took competitive examinations for all types of civil-service positions; 1,625 appealed their grades to the director, who changed 151 grades. Then 1,269 appealed their grades to the Civil Service Commission, which changed 755 grades.[43]

(6) The appointing authority (mayor, city manager, or police chief) can choose from among the top three names on the list. Although his decision is final and unappealable, the appointing authority must give the director of civil service his reasons for so doing if he takes a person other than the top one on the list. Eligibility lists are valid for two years.[44]

(7) Following appointment to a civil-service position, there is a six-month probationary period during which the appointing authority can discharge a man simply by notifying him and the director of civil service why his work was deemed unsatisfactory.[45]

(8) After the probationary period has expired, no person un-

41. Mass. G.L. Ch. 31 §23.
42. Mass. G.L. Ch. 31 §12A.
43. Massachusetts Division of Civil Service, *1962 Annual Report to the Director of Civil Service* (1963), p. 81.
44. Mass. G.L. Ch. 31 §§15, 15C.
45. Mass. G.L. Ch. 31 §20D.

der civil service can be "discharged, removed, suspended for a period exceeding five days, laid off, transferred from such office or employment without his consent, lowered in rank or compensation, nor shall his office or position be abolished, except for just cause and for reasons specifically given him in writing." Such persons have a right to a hearing before the appointing authority and may then ask for a hearing before a member of the Civil Service Commission or his representative and, finally, may appeal to the courts. The requirement of "just cause" and the provisions for a hearing and a right of appeal also apply when a police chief assigns punishment duty (unpaid work) to a police officer. When the appointing authority suspends a man for five days or less, however, he is entitled to notice and a hearing; there is no requirement of just cause.[46]

As will be seen, Massachusetts police forces vary greatly not only in their traffic-law enforcement activities, but also in the norms and conduct of the men and the manner in which they do their work. If state agencies control appointments, promotions, and dismissals in local departments, I shall conclude this chapter by asking which aspects of a police department's incentive system—the set of inducements offered to elicit certain responses from employees[47]—remain under the control of local officials and police chiefs. Since the *informal* division of authority between a police chief and elected local officials varies from city to city and from town to town, at this point I shall only describe the available incentives.

Salaries, fringe benefits, and the length of the work week are

46. Mass. G.L. Ch. 31 §§43, 45.

47. See Chester Barnard, *The Functions of the Executive* (Cambridge: Harvard University Press, 1938); and James G. March and Herbert A. Simon, *Organizations* (New York: Wiley, 1958).

determined by local elected officials. Bills to establish a state-wide minimum salary for policemen have never been passed by the legislature; the top pay for a city patrolman (after serving so many years) varied in 1964 from $4,500 to $6,950.[48]

As mentioned earlier, a police chief may suspend a man for five days or less without proving just cause, although he must provide opportunity for a hearing and must state his reasons for suspending the man.[49]

The nature and extent of police training and retraining programs are largely determined locally. Police chiefs who are willing to pay living expenses can send their men to tuition-free training schools (for new recruits or senior officers) sponsored by the Massachusetts State Police and the FBI. These and other organizations (such as the Northwestern University Traffic Institute) also sponsor periodic seminars on such special subjects as traffic engineering, first aid, riot control, and constitutional law. Apart from these programs, police training has been carried out either through locally operated training academies or simply by assigning a new recruit to an older officer for instruction.[50]

The police chief is generally free to define the duties of his men (the number of blocks to be patrolled, the frequency with which a man must report to headquarters, the length of coffee breaks, and so on) and to assign men to different posts. The chief thus can transfer a patrolman from the day to the night shift,

48. See, e.g., Massachusetts Legislature, House Bill No. 2075 (1963). Mass. G.L. Ch. 41 §108E, added by *Acts of 1959*, Ch. 228, provides that the minimum salary for patrolmen shall be $5,500, but the section is applicable only to such cities and towns as shall vote to accept it.

49. Mass. G.L. Ch. 31 §43(g).

50. As of January 1, 1966, all local policemen are required to attend a police training academy within one year after joining a police force. Mass. G.L. Ch. 41 §96B, added by *Acts of 1964*, Ch. 564.

from a pleasant residential beat to a tough section of the city, or from the detective squad to a traffic post at a busy intersection.

The chief is also free to assign, in any way he deems appropriate, tasks to produce extra income for his men. These include overtime work and pay details, when an outside person pays the department for extra police protection—as at a construction site, a wedding, or a department-store sale. For either kind of work, a policeman will receive pay that is in addition to his regular salary.

Finally, a police chief can attempt to induce certain types of conduct through such informal devices as commending exemplary conduct, paying attention to the public and private activities of his men, and so forth.

2 / Lynn: Leniency in a Residual Police Function

The Chief told me to see Officer O'Donnell, the man who wrote the most traffic tickets on his force. I asked the officer at the desk where I might find O'Donnell. "He's over at the Square." "Would I find him if I drove through at 80 m.p.h.?" I asked. "Hell, you'd find O'Donnell if you were going 21 m.p.h." (The speed limit is 20 m.p.h.) "What's with O'Donnell," I asked. "is he some kind of a nut about traffic?" "No," the desk officer replied, "he's just a good cop." The smile on the officer's face suggested that to be a good cop on the Lynn police force was to be slightly foolish, if not actually to be asking for unnecessary trouble.[1]

If Officer O'Donnell did not understand the situation, the other members of the Lynn Police Department certainly did. In 1964, 184 Lynn policemen issued slightly over 500 tickets for moving violations—an average of 2.7 tickets per police officer and 11.9 per thousand motor vehicles. By way of comparison, the Waltham Police Department, although only about one half as big as the Lynn force, issued almost 5,000 tickets—49.0 tickets per officer and 158.3 per thousand motor vehicles. Why did the Lynn department write fewer tickets than any other force of its size in the state, fewer than some forces one tenth its size? Let us start with

1. The names given to all policemen in this book, other than police chiefs, are fictitious.

a brief description of the city and its politics, and then turn to the enforcement of traffic laws.

Lynn is an old industrial city with politics stressing the caretaker philosophy discussed in my introduction. Located twelve miles east of Boston, its 1960 population was 94,478. Like many other New England manufacturing towns, it grew rapidly in the nineteenth century and declined slowly in the twentieth. The shoe and leather industries, the heart of the Lynn economy, have been gradually dying or leaving the area. Sixty percent of Lynn's labor force today works in manufacturing; Lynn branches of nation-wide corporations produce transportation equipment and electrical and other machinery. General Electric, the largest industry in Lynn, employs 13,000 persons in two plants.[2] Lynn's population is composed primarily of workers in local factories; most of the upper-middle-class and upper-income people employed in Lynn choose to live in surrounding suburbs. In recent years, elected officials have generally been local professional men, owners or managers of small businesses, or employees of General Electric. The present mayor, first elected in 1961, was for twenty years the treasurer of the electrical workers' local union; his predecessor and the present president of the city council were also employed by General Electric.

In matters of state and national politics, Lynn is strongly Democratic. Sixty-five percent of the voters were for Kennedy in 1960; eighty-four percent supported Johnson in 1964. Mayors for the

2. Data on the population, housing, and economy of the cities and towns surveyed in this book are based upon the 1960 U.S. Census of Population and the 1959 Census of Housing and from information submitted to the Massachusetts Division of Employment Security. The Massachusetts Department of Commerce, located in Boston, annually publishes monographs collecting this information for each city and town in the state. For data on the City of Lynn, see Massachusetts Department of Commerce, Division of Research, *Monograph No. 56: City of Lynn* (1962).

last fifteen years, and nine of the eleven councilors elected in 1963, have been registered Democrats. But in the nonpartisan local elections local issues seem to predominate over party affiliation. A former city councilor likened Lynn's politics to those of a small town: "To get elected in my ward," he recalled, "I had to knock on every door and promise better police protection and more playgrounds, sidewalks, and street lights." The present mayor felt that he was being judged solely on his ability to keep taxes down. His 1961 campaign was based only on economy—that if elected he would not spend a nickel more than was absolutely necessary. In a state like Massachusetts, in which cities and town rely almost exclusively on property taxes, this is a fairly common concern of public officials. In Lynn, however, this quest for economy and its caretaker politics seem pervasive. To every question raised about the Lynn Police Department (such as, Why not purchase radar or walkie-talkies? Why not raise salaries to attract better men?), city-hall officials responded: "It's too expensive. We'd have to raise taxes."

Other groups in Lynn also stress its caretaker government and low-tax philosophy. The only daily newspaper eschews the support of anything involving higher taxes. Apart from social and service groups, there are almost no significant city-wide organizations. Women in Lynn who want good government have to journey to a suburb to find a League of Women Voters. The secretary of the Chamber of Commerce recited some local doggerel: "When they are young, they play kick the can; when they grow up, they play kick the Chamber of Commerce." For aspiring Lynn politicians, this can be a fairly cost-free sport—most of the owners and managers of Lynn's businesses live safely outside the city limits and thus cannot vote.

Lynn has had a long history of close ties between city hall and the police department. Under the city charter adopted in 1917, the police department was to be under the supervision of the mayor. Although there was a chief of police, the mayor, in addition to controlling the police budget and making all appointments, actually directed police operations, setting policy and assigning men to shifts and locations in the city. In 1947, however, voters, at the request of the mayor, amended the charter to provide that the police department would be under the supervision of the chief of police.[3]

Today, the formal powers of the mayor with regard to the police are limited to budget control and appointment of men to different ranks on the force. Since 1939, the police force, including the position of chief, has been under the state civil-service system. Although they may choose from among the top three applicants, Lynn mayors have for thirty years adopted a policy of automatically selecting the top man on the examination list. The other formal power of the mayor lies in preparing the police budget; after consultation with his police chief, he submits an annual budget to the council, which may reduce but not increase individual items.

The actual relationship between elected officials and the Lynn police is more extensive than these formal powers might suggest. The city council regularly "directs" the police department to take certain actions. The most frequent directives stem from citizens' complaints and concern such matters as excessive speeding on certain streets or a rash of vagrancy, muggings, or purse snatchings in certain areas. Annually, at the suggestion of downtown merchants, the council will direct the police to ignore parking-meter violations. For two weeks preceding Christmas, the police give meter violators a red and green "Merry Christmas

3. Massachusetts Legislature, *Acts of 1947*, Ch. 107.

Tag"—"You have incurred a Traffic Violation . . . but . . . *Don't Worry*—in the Spirit of Christmas and in Cooperation with the Chamber of Commerce, our Christmas gift to You is *No Violation.* We'd like to have you shop in Lynn again. Merry Christmas!" Although the 1947 charter amendment placed supervision of the force under the chief, and although it might seem that many of these directives involve "supervision," no one could remember any of the three men who had served as chief over the past ten years saying no to a council directive.

The Lynn Police Department is located in an old building adjacent to the district court and the city hall. In 1964, the force consisted of 150 patrolmen, 34 officers, and an assortment of clerks, policewomen, matrons, and mechanics. The chief estimated that over 50 percent of his men had been born or raised in Lynn; he thought that most of his men had completed high school; a few had attended college, and two or three had completed college. The chief's education was limited to completion of high school in neighboring Everett. The 1964 pay scales in the Lynn department were about average for Massachusetts forces of this size; top pay for patrolmen was $6,300; the chief received $9,360. There are no department rules against moonlighting; one member of the force thought that at least half of the force had second jobs; the only restriction seems to be that the outside work cannot conflict with police hours.

Training of new men on the Lynn force takes place on a fairly haphazard basis. After passing the civil-service examinations, successful applicants are placed in the reserve force, doing part-time work such as directing traffic. After working their way up on the reserve list, men are eligible for full-time positions as they open up, although the first six months as a full-time officer are considered a probationary period. During this time the deputy chief conducts informal classes, instructing the new men in law, marksmanship, and such. Instruction in traffic-law enforcement is based on a turgidly worded book of traffic laws ("No person shall operate a motor vehicle at a rate of speed greater than is reasonable and proper . . .") issued by the Registry of Motor Vehicles. Although the state police operate an academy to which municipal forces may send men for six-week training courses, the Lynn force itself prefers to provide basic instruction. Later in their careers, the more promising officers are sent to the academy. Ten or twelve present members of the force have attended this academy; one captain has also attended the FBI national academy in Washington. The present chief attended neither academy.

If one tries to ascertain which members of the Lynn force are involved in traffic-law enforcement, the internal structure of the department becomes somewhat unclear. The organization chart contained in the chief's annual report is only a starting point. Listed under "Traffic Division" are a "captain in charge" (actually the commander of the day shift) and a lieutenant and sergeant of traffic. Other specified posts include two men who investigate traffic accidents, a uniformed clerk who processes parking violations, and several uniformed men who maintain and collect receipts from the city's parking meters. Four men, at irregular intervals, are detailed to give safety talks in the public schools.

At this point in my inquiry, I had to repeat my question—who enforces traffic laws? Four patrolmen, it appears, are formally assigned to traffic duty. Each is given an area of the business district to patrol, directing traffic at busy intersections, giving information to motorists, and writing tickets for parking violations. There are also between ten and twenty officers who man street crossings at schools and factory gates at rush hours.

I felt that I had to try once more. "I understand about direct-ing traffic and helping pedestrians. Who is it, though, that is assigned to enforcing the laws? Who goes looking for violators? Who writes the citations?" "Why, we all do—every man walking a route, every man in a car is looking for traffic violations." To understand how traffic-law enforcement is organized in the Lynn Police Department, then, we have to think of it as a "residual" function—something you do when you are not doing something else. Each man on duty—the men walking routes and the men in cruisers—is told to work in a specified area of the city. The men on routes will assist motorists, check parking meters, harass loi-terers, or chase shoplifters. The men in cruisers will answer calls about prowlers, check vacant homes, or deliver expectant mothers to hospitals. When they are not doing any one of these things, Lynn policemen are "on traffic." The reasons for and conse-quences on this arrangement will be discussed shortly.

This haphazard situation is repeated if we attempt to trace the process of recording a moving-traffic violation. The Registry of Motor Vehicles citations (tickets) which were described in Chap-ter One are kept in the police station. All officers—both route men and those in cars—are given unnumbered slips with spaces for recording the facts needed to complete a Registry citation. When an officer completes his tour of duty, or on the following day, he will leave any completed slips on the desk of the lieutenant in charge of traffic, Lieutenant Lee. "When enough have come in to keep a typist busy" (but by law within three days of the viola-tion), the slips are copied onto Registry citation forms. The rec-ommendation (warning, Registry action, or court) is made by the captain in charge of the day shift or by Lee if the captain does not happen to be around.

What traffic violations are ticketed in Lynn? The 1964 annual report of the chief listed some 550 violations leading to about 500 Registry citations (multiple charges against a motorist, such as speeding accompanied by driving under the influence, can be recorded on a single citation form). Of these violations, 211, or 38 percent, were minor violations—speeding, stop signs, red lights. The remaining 62 percent were for serious offenses: 116 driving under the influence, 67 using a motor vehicle without authority (joy riding), 43 operating without a license, 25 leaving the scene of an accident, 22 unregistered cars, 23 driving while license is suspended. This high proportion of serious offenses in a regular feature of Lynn ticketing—55 percent in 1957, 44 percent in 1962, and 69 percent in 1963, to take a few recent years.[4] In Cambridge, by contrast, a far greater amount of ticket writing occurred, but the increase was concentrated in the minor offenses. In random samples (about one in three) of tickets written by the Cambridge department in 1964, 88 percent of the force's tickets dealt with speeding, stop signs, and the like. (The implication is, of course, clear: any police force will write tickets for serious violations; the forces *interested* in traffic will also write tickets for minor violations.)

This, then, is the picture of traffic-law enforcement in Lynn—the force is not organized to maximize traffic enforcement (at least in the sense of ticketing violators), the men produce few tickets, and most of the tickets written are for serious offenses. Why? Let us first consider a few supposedly rational explanations. One was offered by several members of the Lynn Police Department—moving violations are not a serious problem simply because it is physically difficult to violate a traffic law. Lynn's

4. Indicative of the somewhat slipshod recordkeeping in the Lynn Police Department, these were the only years for which department annual reports were available.

streets, they argued, are so narrow and winding that there are few places where a motorist can build up a high rate of speed. The only difficulty with this explanation is that on personal observation, at least, Lynn's streets are not particularly narrower or more tortuous than those of Cambridge or Waltham, where ten times as many tickets were written in 1964.[5] (I do not claim that as many violations occurred in Lynn as in these other cities, but merely that Lynn did not have as few as one tenth as many.)

A second explanation for the low number of tickets in Lynn might have something to do with the local district court. Police officers are required to appear in the Lynn court when their traffic cases are scheduled to be heard; they cannot wait to learn if the motorist will plead not guilty before coming to court. Officers mentioned a few specific grievances—that the fines should be higher for more serious offenses (say, a motorist going through the center of the city at 80 m.p.h.), that the judge was being too protective of the defendant's rights, and so on. In addition to the fact that the Lynn judge levies fines of the same magnitude as other judges in the state, and in addition to the fact that his conviction rate (about 98 percent) is similar to that of other judges, two other facts weaken this explanation. First, ticketing in Lynn is different from ticketing in Cambridge and Waltham—not in the serious offenses, where the fines are supposedly not high enough, but in the minor offenses, where the Lynn chief (correctly) assumed that his judge was fining at about the same rate as other judges. Second, in several cities where chiefs objected vociferously either to court procedures or to the judge's sentences, the dissatisfaction was manifested in the

5. Unfortunately, there are no objective measures of the quality of a city's street system which would permit analysis of the likelihood of traffic violations.

recommendations made on tickets, not in the number of tickets written. The chief in Cambridge, for example, marked 77 percent of his 1964 tickets (other than those given warnings) for Registry rather than court action. In Lynn, by contrast, a study of 1964 ticket recommendations showed 48 warnings, 226 court summonses, 162 arrests, and only 5 requests for Registry action.

If these "rational" explanations are unsatisfactory, what is left? The answer lies simply in a basic lack of interest in traffic-law enforcement. Evidence of this attitude was omnipresent in the Lynn Police Department: when asked why men were not specifically assigned to traffic-law enforcement, officers would say either, "we haven't got enough men to do our routine work, let alone traffic duties," or "there isn't much speeding in Lynn, and I can't afford to put a man out by a stop sign to catch a few violators." These conclusions about inability to handle traffic did not seem to come from any particular plan of action—whenever citizens' calls or council directives came in, the force had enough men to spare one for, say, selective enforcement at Main and Central streets. Whether the force has enough men for traffic on a given day depends on whether traffic is a residual function (almost always) or a specific issue (as it is whenever the council or citizens demand a crackdown at a particular intersection). Since no one is specifically assigned to traffic enforcement on a regular basis, allocation of men to traffic work will come in response to, rather than in anticipation of, complaints. Since traffic violations do not produce complaints at the same rate or intensity as, say, drunks or prowlers or shoplifters, this residual policy leads to a constant deferral of traffic in order to handle "more important" matters.

A corollary of this lack of interest in traffic brings up the matter of the norms of the Lynn Police Department: the men on the force are not encouraged to write tickets, and in several ways they are actually discouraged from writing them. First, since traffic for every officer (except the one who is sent to Main and Central when Mrs. Brown complains) is only a residual duty, he has no reason to produce a quota of tickets to prove he was on the job that day. Although a superior officer could (but does not) "tail" a parking-meter officer to see if every car in front of an expired meter has a ticket, there is no equally easy way to prove that Officer X saw a moving violation and did not write a ticket.

Second, the traffic record of an officer does not seem to be involved, in any positive way, in his promotion or assignment within the department. Promotions are determined solely by civil-service examination grades; the chiefs never seem to have tried to persuade the mayor to take one rather than another of the top three men on the basis of his record. ("Never have tried" is perhaps unfair in the light of the announced policy of Lynn mayors of taking the top candidate regardless of record.) A more accessible tool for discipline is the assignment of men to undesirable shifts or duties. Working on the graveyard shift or having to haul drunks out of bars are admittedly unprestigious posts, but there was no evidence that a Lynn patrolman was ever so punished for failing to write traffic tickets. The chief said that a man who did not write parking tickets would be transferred to another post, but (a) "not writing parking tickets" seems to be determined by a merchant's complaints that his customers cannot find parking spaces (a situation that can be avoided by an enlightened officer who will write a few tickets for the merchant), and (b) the transfer would not necessarily involve a punishment detail. Asked why some men write fewer tickets than others, the chief laconically replied, "Some men are less interested in traffic than others"; he would transfer such men to posts and duties in which they would have more interest.

While *not* writing tickets usually will not get a Lynn policeman into trouble, writing tickets can; it seems that a Lynn policeman is more likely to get into trouble for a ticket wrongly written (as defined below) than for a deserved ticket not written. The stories told of punishment arising from traffic matters were stories of excessive zeal rather than of laziness. When asked if new men are instructed on how to appraise traffic violations (say that a ticket should be written every time a motorist exceeds the speed limit by so many miles per hour), the chief said, "No, we just want our men to use common sense. We only want our men to write tickets when the violation is beyond a reasonable doubt." Common sense, discretion, and understanding of the public are more highly valued norms than "hustling" or "go-getting."

In case an exceptionally obtuse officer is still in doubt about whether to err in the direction of zeal or moderation, he might recall the attitude of a former Lynn chief. This chief said that if a patrolman were to write a ticket when a motorist was driving 50 m.p.h. by the city park (on a two-lane street in the center of the city), the chief would summon the patrolman into his office. "Well, did you ask *why* he was going fifty? Did you find out if he was late for work? Maybe his wife was sick . . ."

A final explanation of Lynn ticketing policies concerns the matter of leadership or discipline. For the last eight years, the Lynn Police Department has been led by men who, although regarded as outstanding police officers earlier in their careers, were unremarkable in their years as chief.[6] The chiefs who assumed control in 1957 and 1962, having achieved the top grades

6. For a few months in 1961, a deputy chief was made acting chief. The comments made here about the permanent chiefs since 1957 are not intended to apply to him, since his term in office was too short to permit analysis.

on the civil-service examinations, were both physically infirm and in their early sixties. Having only a few years to serve, neither felt called upon to become "movers and shakers," to take the chance of making enemies. The chief appointed in early 1964 is physically healthy and slightly younger (fifty-eight when appointed) but probably will not choose to change things very much. He is and wants to be a "nice guy"; when asked if he handles traffic like chiefs in neighboring cities and towns (which, unknown to him, produced from two to seven times as many tickets per thousand motor vehicles in 1964), he cheerfully replied, "I hope I do."

Unfortunately, it is impossible to determine whether the "weak" chiefs after 1957 in fact handled traffic any more leniently than their predecessors, whom everyone referred to almost wistfully as tough chiefs; no annual reports are available for the years before 1957. Incidents of toughness ascribed to these chiefs involved matters of personal character and willingness to say no to the mayor and council; no one knew if they were tough about the writing of tickets. There has been little variation among the three later chiefs—for the years 1957 and 1961 through 1964 (no reports were available for 1958 through 1960), the number of traffic tickets written in each year was 764, 470, 372, 509, and 554.

From the point of view of a motorist in Lynn, then, he is unlikely to be stopped by a policeman, and if stopped he is unlikely to get a ticket. Most outsiders interviewed—city-hall officials, city councilors, civic leaders—seemed fairly satisfied with the way the Lynn Police Department conducts its affairs. Merchants and the Chamber of Commerce wished that the police would be more active in enforcing parking laws (except during the Christmas season, when they ask the police to substitute the "Merry Christmas tags" for parking tickets). One official of a large local industry said that the Lynn police have been quite cooperative in directing rush-hour traffic and in handling labor disputes. His only complaint was that the Lynn force does not have a riot squad especially trained for crowd control.

Apart from these mild suggestions for upgrading the Lynn Police Department, its policies have met with general approval. As a former mayor said, the main thing that Lynn citizens want from the police department is a feeling of security. In handling traffic violations, one city councilor felt that the most important thing is for a policeman to display understanding—a recognition that there are certain cases in which a traffic violation should be overlooked. "We are proud of our policemen," one city official said, "because they use discretion—they know that they should give a motorist a lecture instead of a ticket if the offense is not too serious."

3 / Waltham: Pleasing All of the People All of the Time

Is Waltham altogether too complacent a city?

And is this complacency the breeding ground for a form of downtown blight that is threatening its economy? Yes is the answer on both points. Waltham pats itself on the back frequently as it contemplates the $50 million-plus Route 128 complex. It swells with pride over Brandeis' growth, the imminent establishment of Bentley College, fine new residential property, a new $2.5 million municipal center . . . We get the feeling the community is coasting along, self-satisfied with the apparent stability (of municipal affairs).

—Editorial in *Waltham*
News-Tribune, December 30, 1964

The people of Waltham have had a good excuse for being self-satisfied, for Waltham has been one of the few cities in Massachusetts to make a successful transition from a mill town in the nineteenth century to a center for electronics industries in the 1950s and 1960s. During the nineteenth century, the Charles River attracted a number of textile, iron, and other manufacturing firms to Waltham. In the years after World War II, Waltham acquired a new industrial base. With the completion in 1952 of Route 128 (a circumferential highway around Boston) along the western edge of the city, many acres of Waltham farmland have been transformed into industrial parks. Major industries today include Polaroid, Sylvania, Raytheon, and Clevite. Between 1930 and 1960, Waltham's population grew from 40,000 to 55,000—an increase of 41 percent—while the Boston metropolitan area as a whole grew by only 19 percent. Waltham residents today are basically a homeowning, middle- and lower-middle-class group; extremes of either poverty or wealth are rare.[1]

The basic philosophy of most people active in Waltham politics seems to be a moderate, consensus version of the program of the Waltham Chamber of Commerce: continued efforts to attract new industry to the Route 128 area, support for Waltham's downtown shopping area in the face of competition from Boston and suburban shopping centers, and generally "making Waltham a nice place to live." In recent years, the Chamber has been more representative of the local retail merchants than of the newer electronics industries; as the executive director of the Chamber said, "There appears to be a lack of attachment and a lack of understanding and interest in local affairs among these new business leaders. They appear to be more Boston-orientated than Waltham-orientated."[2]

The other major voice in Waltham affairs is the daily *Waltham News-Tribune,* the only newspaper in the city. The *News-Tribune* has been a vigorous supporter of civic improvement; its managing editor was vice-chairman of a fourteen-community committee that worked to bring about completion of Route 128 in 1952. Concluding the editorial with which this chapter began, the *News-Tribune* attacked the complacency and self-satisfaction of Wathamites and called for interest in long-range planning, down-

1. Data on the population and economy of Waltham are from Massachusetts Department of Commerce, Division of Research, *Monograph No. 79: City of Waltham* (1964).

2. Theodore L. Manning, "A Proposed Program of Work for the Waltham Chamber of Commerce" (1965).

town urban renewal, and the like. The paper, however, has generally avoided any radical reform or crusading policies. As its managing editor explained, "When you've grown up with city officials, you don't go after them unless you feel things are *too* bad. You try to look at the city in a broad sense and hammer away at the things that need doing—you seldom go after individuals."

Since 1957, under the leadership of Mayor Austin Rhodes, a retired Waltham factory executive and former president of the Chamber of Commerce, Waltham politics have been based on a low-keyed consensus approach to the economic-growth philosophy outlined in the introduction. During the eight years of the Rhodes administration, Walthamites were hard put to name any local controversies, other than a dispute over whether to expand the high school at its present site or to build a second school at a new location. One city councilor said that getting elected was simply a matter of being known around the community; rather than choosing among candidates on the basis of issues, Walthamites simply look for a "reasonably intelligent man."

Many councilors and outside observers have noted in the Rhodes administration an era of good feeling among the mayor's office, the city council, and the various city departments. Rhodes usually consults with the council before announcing new policies. City employees, including the police, have received raises every two years since Rhodes took office; in 1965 the top patrolman's salary rose from $4,500 in 1956 to $6,000. Several councilors mentioned that policemen no longer call them about requests for raises; since raises have been coming through so regularly, the chief insists that his men should let well enough alone. Rhodes has always accepted the recommendations for appointments of his department heads, who take the top names on civil-service examination lists. (His predecessor had skipped two men in 1956 to appoint the present police chief.) Generally, Rhodes has left his department heads free to run their own departments. As one man closely associated with Rhodes put it, "This has not been an administration marked by executive influence." Most increases in the city budget have been devoted to extending basic municipal services—water, sewers, schools, and streets—to the new residential areas and to replacing old municipal buildings; in 1964, a $2.5 million complex was completed to house the police, fire, and public-works departments. Although he added a city planner (his former administrative assistant) to his staff in 1962, Rhodes has not been interested in comprehensive zoning or urban-renewal proposals.

On paper, the Waltham Police Department looks like a smaller version of the Lynn force. In 1964, the Waltham force had one hundred men and officers. Except for a detective bureau and a traffic bureau, the patrolmen are simply assigned to different work shifts. The traffic bureau in Waltham, as in Lynn, handles traffic engineering, accident investigation, and the processing of traffic tickets; it contains no traffic-enforcement men. As in Lynn, Waltham policemen do not carry Registry ticket books but are given unnumbered forms on which to record information about traffic violations. The chief decides what recommendation will be made and forwards the ticket to the traffic bureau, where the information is transferred to Registry ticket forms or court complaints are prepared.

The 1965 chief of the Waltham Police Department took office in 1956. Following the retirement of Chief Asa McKenna, a civil-service examination was held to fill the position. First on the resulting list was Joseph Cunningham, who had been serving as acting chief for eight months. But the mayor at that time, Paul Shaughnessy, skipped Cunningham and the second man to take the third-ranked applicant, William Carmody. Carmody was a Waltham man who had only recently been promoted to the rank of provisional captain. He was also a life-long friend of Mayor Shaughnessy's, and observers attributed the appointment to friendship rather than to any judgment on the policies or abilities of the three men.

Walthamites remember Chief McKenna as a strict man, a tough chief (his policy of enforcing traffic laws against buses precipitated a protest strike by bus drivers in the late 1940s); the universal opinion of Bill Carmody is that he is a "nice guy." McKenna, councilors remembered, "wouldn't give you the time of day"; but Carmody would always "slap you on the back and call you by your first name." One councilor thought it significant that Carmody was a good family man, one who understands people. Merchants speak of Carmody's cooperation in providing police protection in the business district; as in Lynn, the Waltham police give Santa Claus tags to parking violators during the Christmas shopping season. In 1963, several weeks after the city council had imposed a parking ban on one street in the shopping district, Carmody asked that it be lifted because he felt it was harming local merchants.[3] When Brandeis University students get into trouble with the law, Carmody tries to settle things quietly and without publicity.

Some Walthamites, while admitting the appropriateness of the nice-guy description of Carmody, have some doubts about his direction of the police department. "The police department," said one man who had watched both McKenna and Carmody in

3. "Council Ends Complete Moody St. Parking Ban," *Waltham News-Tribune,* July 16, 1963.

action, "has an 'Alice in Wonderland' atmosphere about it now. Talking to Carmody, you'd never know crimes are committed in Waltham. Sure, he's a nice guy, but since when is a police chief supposed to be a nice guy? Carmody is totally miscast as a cop, to say nothing of as a police chief." Reporters assigned to cover the Waltham department find it difficult to get access to crime records in the police desk book. Carmody, they say, tries to cover up outbreaks of burglary or vandalism, and to avoid arresting many people who have been apprehended.

Several councilors think that the sweetness and light of Carmody's demeanor is an attempt to gloss over deficiencies in the department. One recalled that Carmody was "touchy" on an occasion when several councilors dropped over to headquarters unannounced to check on conditions. During budget hearings, another councilor tried to encourage Carmody to send more of his men to the state training academy; Carmody replied that his policy of sending senior officers to special seminars on police matters was adequate education; so new recruits are simply instructed by other men on the force. In recent years, the council has also tried to increase the size of the police force (it grew from 59 men in 1950 to its present size of 100 in 1960), but Carmody prefers to give overtime pay to his regular men. During the 1965 budget hearings, Carmody asked for $90,000 for overtime work; the council renewed its offer to appoint more men and chopped $25,000 off the amount requested for overtime.

All parallels between the traffic activities of the Lynn and Waltham police departments end abruptly when we look at the number of traffic tickets written in 1964. The 184 men on the Lynn force, it may be remembered, ticketed 502 persons in 1964 —an average of 2.7 persons per police officer and 11.9 per thousand motor vehicles. The hundred men on the Waltham police force ticketed 4,901 persons—49.0 per police officer and 158.3 per thousand motor vehicles. To a certain extent, this policy of strict enforcement predates Carmody's appointment as chief, as is shown in Table 10.

Although the Waltham Police Department under Chief Carmody is reported by outsiders to be somewhat more active in the area of traffic enforcement than it was under Chief McKenna, the

Table 10. Ticketing in Waltham, 1950–1964

Chief	Year	Tickets	Tickets per 1,000 motor vehicles
Asa McKenna	1950	407	25.1
(1938-1955)	1951	721	41.8
	1952	n.a.	n.a.
	1953	3,126	164.4
	1954	1,423	72.5
Acting chief	1955	407	24.1
William Carmody	1956	1,138	52.5
(1956–1966)	1957	1,439	64.8
	1958	4,615	207.0
	1959	5,737	234.9
	1960	3,454	130.6
	1961	3,656	134.4
	1962	3,843	132.8
	1963	4,337	140.1
	1964	5,633	182.0

Note. Since the Waltham Police Department records each traffic violation on a separate ticket, the totals presented in the Tickets column reflect violations rather than violators. In other cities, multiple violations are recorded on a single ticket. When cities are being compared with each other, all figures are transcribed to the "violators" form. Here, where different years in one city are being compared, the department's figures (violations) are used, divided by the number of vehicles registered in each year in the city; thus the 1964 figure in this table (182.0) is larger than the figure used in the text (158.3), which is based upon the number of violators.

difference is not as great as these figures suggest. First, it should be remembered that between 1950 and 1960, Waltham's population increased by 17 percent, and the construction of new industries along Route 128 added even more to the traffic volume on the city's streets. Second, the police department increased in size from fifty-nine men in 1950 to one hundred in the years since 1959. Finally, with reference to the decline in the number of tickets reported for 1954 and 1955, it might be noted that McKenna felt that the district court judge (appointed in 1952) was being too lenient with traffic violators. As a result, although his interest in *apprehending* traffic violators remained, McKenna began to send many cases directly to the Registry for action. Since the present ticket system, in which requests for Registry action are written on the same ticket form as cases going to court, did not begin until 1962, the Registry phase of McKenna's work is not reflected by the figures contained in this table and the Registry figures are, unfortunately, unavailable.

In ascertaining why so many more traffic tickets (both absolutely and per thousand motor vehicles) were written in Waltham than in Lynn, there seem to be few factors other than deliberate policies of the two departments which might explain the difference. Lynn had a higher number of police officers per thousand population (1.99) than Waltham (1.72); so it is hard to say that the Lynn department was understaffed and therefore less well-equipped to handle traffic. The average number of traffic accidents of all types between 1961 and 1963 was lower in Waltham than in Lynn, both absolutely (909 as against 1,290) and relatively (34.3 per thousand motor vehicles in Waltham as against 35.9 in Lynn); this would not seem to provide a source of outside pressure for strict enforcement in Waltham. (The possibility that police ticketing policies are related to accident rates in

any way—either that a high accident rate leads to a strict enforcement policy or that a strict enforcement policy leads to a
low accident rate—will be discussed in Chapter Seven.)

No organized groups or political leaders in Waltham seem to
have pushed for a strict enforcement policy. The Chamber of
Commerce and the *News-Tribune* have been interested in traffic,
but only insofar as parking and ease of reaching the business
district are concerned. Relations between city hall and police
headquarters were equally relaxed in Waltham and in Lynn;
whereas Waltham's mayor and councilors were generally proud
of the enforcement record of their police, they all disclaimed
credit for encouraging it, and several councilors expressed a hope
that the police might relax a little bit.

The judges in both the Lynn and Waltham district courts
levied traffic fines (usually $5 or $10 for first offenders charged
with minor violations) which were generally lower than the uniform fines set up in 1965, when pay-by-mail was established on a
state-wide basis. The Waltham court, however, did have one
policy that significantly distinguished it from the Lynn court. In
Waltham, the officer who writes a ticket is ordered to appear in
court only after a motorist pleads not guilty; a Lynn officer must
appear when the case is first called. Chief Carmody said that he
would not be able to send as many violators to court if the judges
were to require the earlier appearance—it might tie up half of
his force during court hours. Although the policy of a court
regarding the appearance of an officer may be a necessary condition for a strict enforcement policy, it does not seem to be a
sufficient condition—while the Waltham police were ticketing
158 persons per thousand motor vehicles in 1964, the other two
forces in the Waltham court district were ticketing many fewer
persons—74 persons per thousand vehicles in Weston (popula-

tion 8,261) and 34 in Watertown (population 39,092).

Within the Waltham Police Department, there are also few factors to distinguish it from the Lynn department. Promotions are based solely on civil-service examinations, and transfers from the night shift to the more desirable day shift are based solely on seniority. Overtime work is distributed fairly evenly among all patrolmen who ask for it. As in the case of Officer O'Donnell in Lynn, Waltham policemen who frequently write traffic tickets are subjected to a moderate amount of ridicule by other members of the force. Two men who had been manning a traffic car since 1958 mentioned that other policemen refer to them as the "Gold-dust Twins" and stage-whisper "Car 54, where are you?" when they enter the station; comic strips depicting overzealous traffic officers appear on the squad-room bulletin board with the two men's names written in. One Waltham lieutenant, who thought the department's ticketing drive somewhat silly, said that he counseled new men to "slow down. If the chief sees you writing tickets and *then* you start to slow down, they'll notice the change and be after you. So why ask for trouble?—just play things nice and easy."

If, with the exception of the Waltham court's policy of not requiring officers to appear when traffic cases are first called, the Lynn and Waltham police departments appear to be so similar, what explains the contrast in ticket figures? Why did the Waltham police ticket more than thirteen times as many persons per thousand motor vehicles? The explanation offered by many Walthamites is that their policemen write tickets because they are constantly being pushed to write tickets by Jim Thomas, the captain in charge of the department's traffic bureau. Although both men are about the same age (in their early sixties) and although both men joined the force at the same time (in 1937),

Traffic Captain Thomas and Chief Carmody have very different personalities. Carmody refuses to give the official Registry ticket books to his men; Thomas would like to give out the books. Once, when I was waiting to see Thomas, an old man came in to complain about a stop-sign ticket he had received—his first ticket in fifty years of driving. A lieutenant listened to his story and agreed to dismiss the charges. When told of this, Captain Thomas snorted, "What was he griping about? He ran the stop sign, didn't he?"

Carmody is as accommodating to his men as he is to politicians and local residents; Thomas constantly pushes the men working in the traffic bureau and tries to spur on all men assigned to traffic enforcement even though they are not under his command. When traffic men do not produce as many parking or moving-violation tickets as he thinks they should, Thomas takes it upon himself to harass them and he tries to get the chief to back him up. Once, fed up with the laziness of one man assigned to patrol parking meters, who produced only twenty parking tickets at the end of a day's work, Thomas took a patrolman down to the business district: in ninety minutes, the two men wrote one hundred and fifty parking tickets.

Captain Thomas' crusading spirit, it might be noted, has had a mixed reception in Waltham. Everyone was happy that Waltham's classification for automobile insurance rates has dropped from Territory 11 (with the fourth highest rates in the state) in 1955 to Territory 13 (with the fifth highest rates) in 1965, even though the population and number of cars were steadily rising.[4] Many Walthamites think, however, that Thomas is carrying

4. Massachusetts Department of Banking and Insurance, Division of Insurance, "Classification of Risks and Schedule of Premium Charges" (1955 and 1965).

things a bit too far. "It's ridiculous," one city councilor said, "to give a ticket when a motorist runs a stop sign at 11:00 P.M." Another thought that Thomas was trying to do a good job, but "if we let him carry out all of his wild ideas, it would raise hell with business." A third felt that Thomas' zeal was a source of irritation in the community: "He takes himself too god-damned seriously. He doesn't use discretion in writing tickets. He would do a lot more good if he was more tactful."

It is difficult, however, to attribute the interest shown in writing tickets by Waltham policemen simply to the crusading spirit of their traffic captain, for Thomas is a captain without a ship. Enforcement men report to Chief Carmody, not to Thomas. Rewards (such as good assignments and overtime work) and punishments are distributed by Carmody, not by Thomas. As Thomas testified from personal experience with respect to the men who were supposed to be under his control (patrolmen assigned to type up tickets or investigate accidents), he is powerless to "control" anybody unless Chief Carmody is willing to back him up.

Although Carmody seldom takes the disciplinary actions that Thomas would like, he has at least been interested enough in traffic enforcement to encourage his men to write tickets and has taken a number of men off other assignments in order to work solely on traffic. But we noted earlier that Carmody enjoys the reputation in Waltham of being a nice guy and a good family man. A chief of similar personality in Lynn, I found, felt that being "nice" implied a duty not to push his men and not to alienate local citizens by a policy of strict enforcement. Why is it that Waltham's chief comes to the opposite conclusion from the same set of goals?

In all fairness, it must be stated that Carmody feels that strict traffic enforcement *is* part of being a nice guy. To those who call to complain about a ticket, Carmody will be nice by giving a warning. For all other residents of Waltham, however, Carmody feels that "niceness" implies strict enforcement. "Enforcement is the best way to cut down accidents and insurance rates. If I can keep the people of Waltham alive, I think I've done a good job. What I am supposed to tell parents when their child is run over? That I wanted to be friendly and so didn't push enforcement? You can't be too friendly and be a police chief. The people want enforcement."

Some Walthamites, though, think that Carmody is merely choosing the path of least resistance to pressures put upon him by Captain Thomas. Members of the city council who observed the increase in ticket writing concluded that Carmody was agreeing to most of Thomas' demands while "sitting on him" occasionally for the sake of public relations. The public appearance of harmony between Thomas and Carmody implies to the men on the force that Carmody will back up Thomas' orders, even though the men knew of no instance in which he had reprimanded an officer or reassigned him for reasons related to traffic.

A final explanation, offered by several city councilors, was that Carmody was thin-skinned, "sensitive to criticism." If a councilor complains about the police department's lack of training or about any other policy, these councilors say, Carmody lashes back by pushing ticket writing as proof that his men are on the job. It is hard to say whether this explanation is correct. The ticketing figures show that enforcement has been rather uniformly high since 1958. If Carmody is adopting a strict enforcement policy as a defense mechanism against criticism, he has been doing it on a fairly regular basis, and it is an action that can be equally well explained by other concerns, such as his personal interest in safety and the pressures of Thomas.

Thus, part of the difference between traffic-law enforcement in Lynn and in Waltham can be explained by the fact that two high-ranking officers in the Waltham department *want* tickets written. Even if disciplinary measures are not taken against non-ticketers, the men on the Waltham force know that their superiors would like to see tickets written; the policy we stated by a former Lynn chief—"Well, did you ask this man *why* he was speeding?" —was completely absent in the Waltham Police Department.

The stated desires of Chief Carmody and Captain Thomas to have tickets written are reinforced by the way in which the enforcement function is organized with the Waltham department. In Lynn, it will be recalled, *every* patrolman was "on traffic"— enforcement was a residual function, something every man was supposed to be doing when he was not doing something else. My earlier conclusion was that, since every Lynn policeman could claim he was usually occupied with "something else"—answering calls, giving information, and such—none had to produce traffic tickets as proof that he was on the job.

But in Waltham a number of police officers are assigned *specifically* to traffic enforcement on a long-term basis. Since 1958, one car (two men) has been assigned solely to daytime enforcement work. These two men move around the city checking eight locations at which lines have been painted, one eighth of a mile apart; using stop watches, they time speeders and are under orders to ticket any car traveling at more than 45 m.p.h. in 30 m.p.h. zones. In January 1965, Chief Carmody assigned a second car to daytime enforcement work, although these men are frequently taken off traffic work to answer emergency calls or to fill in for men who are sick. Three nights a week, from 6:00 to 10:00 P.M., two cars are sent out specifically on traffic enforcement; these cars are manned by men from other shifts who are working on an overtime basis. Finally, the chief places a varying number of men at intersections to look for stop-sign violations.

The tickets written in Waltham in the first five months of 1965 showed the importance of these specific traffic assignments. During this period, the Waltham Police Department wrote 5,100 tickets. The two men in the full-time enforcement car wrote 1,326 tickets. The men in the car basically assigned to enforcement but which is also used for emergency calls wrote 567 tickets. A man assigned in February to stop-sign work wrote 1,161 tickets in four months. A sixth man, who was assigned to check locations in the business district at which violations had been reported by citizens, wrote 572 tickets in the five-month period. These six men, then, wrote 3626 tickets, or 71 percent of the department's total in the five-month period. (Since it was impossible to identify the other men who were doing overtime enforcement work, this is not a complete listing of all tickets written by men specifically assigned to traffic work.)

It is interesting to note how these six men were picked for traffic assignments. Although overtime work is usually distributed evenly among the men who want it, Captain Thomas noted that they try to give the enforcement overtime work to men who like writing tickets. "We're putting men out to write tickets. If they don't produce, we're not going to pay for something we're not getting." Still, although the regular enforcement men have been "producing" tickets since they were put on these jobs, it is not clear that they were picked because they had a prior reputation for ticket writing. The chief claimed that in 1958 he had selected two men to man a traffic car "because they were outstanding men, because they were young and aggressive." The men themselves felt that to a certain extent they had been put in a car because their aggressive characters were angering people in the downtown business area, where they had been assigned to parking-meter enforcement. "When I told a driver to move his car, I wanted him to *move* it, and I didn't want any lip out of him," one recalled. The other mentioned that he had been restrained from "flattening" a teenager just before he was transferred to the traffic car. When, in January 1965, Chief Carmody decided to assign a second car to daytime enforcement work, he simply chose the two men on the night shift who were next in line, on the basis of seniority, for daytime work. The patrolman who produced 1,200 stop-sign tickets in four months was given this job simply because of a back injury. As a rookie he had been assigned to the night shift; when he was injured, and was under doctor's orders to do only light work, Carmody told him to watch stop signs from 3:30 to 11:30 P.M. The patrolman who checks stop signs in the business district is an extra man on the day shift, and so he is given traffic assignments whenever he does not have to fill in for men who are sick or on vacation.

Why do these men write tickets? No one stated that he was being pushed by Carmody or by Thomas, although the men in the second enforcement car noted that Thomas was trying to increase their production of tickets by encouraging headquarters to minimize the number of emergency calls that took them off traffic work. In fact, most of the enforcement men said that they liked their assignments because they were *not* being pushed as much as men on other assignments. With the exception of the extra man in the business district who, like other patrolmen, has to report to headquarters at regular intervals and has to be available for reassignment by his sergeant, the enforcement men were on their own. Carmody, one car man explained, "gives us complete authority. We only report to him, not to a sergeant or captain. We go anywhere in the city we want to. We only go to headquarters to pick up the car or to drop off the tickets we've written." For some of these men, the enforcement assignments represented an opportunity to get day work before other daytime assignments came open. "Well," one said, "you might say enforcement is a better job than shaking doorknobs from midnight to 8:00 A.M."

Along with the fact that these men like the hours and the freedom of action which enforcement assignments offer them, the large volume of Waltham tickets can be explained by the concept of "specialization." One of the traffic men used a medical analogy: "In medicine, you don't have general practitioners any more—you have obstetricians, heart men, brain men, and so forth. It's the same way in police work. No officer can know *all* the laws. It's a full-time job just knowing when you can arrest a man or when you have to have a search warrant. So, when I was put on enforcement, I started out reading the motor-vehicle laws from cover to cover. Whenever the newspapers report a change in traffic laws, I cut it out. You have to know what laws to enforce. You have to be a specialist."

To the other enforcement men, the idea of specialization has a somewhat less philosophical meaning. Two men brought in from the night shift put it this way: "Since our only job was going to ticketing, we knew we could stay on days as long as we produced; the chief might put us back on nights if we don't produce." A second patrolman said, "Nobody is pushing to get tickets written; men write tickets when that is their only job." Finally, "I don't care what happens to my tickets. If I write up the violations I've seen, I can sleep nights—I've done my day's work."

These comments show that it is difficult to say whether these men write traffic tickets because they are being pushed. They know that writing tickets is what superior officers (or at least the chief and the traffic captain) expect enforcement specialists to do. They enjoy the enforcement assignments, if only because of the hours and the freedom from direct supervision. And so they write tickets.

4 / Malden: Political Activity
and Complacency

> Urban renewal and redevelopment are perhaps the biggest
> things that ever happened in Malden. Before it, we were a
> seedy city in many respects.
>
> —Editorial in the
> *Malden Evening News*, November 1, 1963

The 1960 Census figures generally bear out this description of
Malden, Massachusetts, as being a seedy city. Socially, economi-
cally, and politically, it seems much like a smaller version of
Lynn. Malden's 1960 population of 57,676 was slightly smaller
than its 1930 population, and most residents are middle- and
lower-middle-class workers in local manufacturing and trade
firms.[1] The *Malden Evening News* and the Chamber of Commerce, both of which stress the economic-growth philosophy
predominant in Waltham, are generally regarded as insignificant
voices in Malden politics. Like Lynn and Waltham, Malden lacks
a resident business-leadership class. This does not stem so much
from a predominance of nation-wide corporations as from the
fact that executives in Malden industries, like those in Waltham
industries, tend to live in surrounding suburbs. An official of the
Malden Chamber of Commerce estimated that 80 percent of the

1. Information on Malden's population and economy is from Massachusetts Department of Commerce, Division of Research, *Monograph No. 110:
City of Malden* (1962).

Malden business community lives outside the city. In recent years, the Chamber has supported a downtown renewal plan, a new city hall, and improvements in traffic conditions, and has sought to attract new business to the city.

Although local officials in Malden have accepted the goal of economic growth to the point of approving two good-sized urban-renewal projects, almost nothing is undertaken which requires expenditures of *local* tax funds. As in Lynn, the caretaker philosophy predominates, and only the most traditional services are provided by the city. Despite repeated *Evening News* and Chamber of Commerce demands for modernization, a brick building that predates the Civil War still serves as Malden's city hall. (As my study was underway, attempts were being made to include a new city hall as part of an urban-renewal plan.) An otherwise popular mayor was voted out of office in 1959 solely because, according to most observers, he raised the tax rate by $12. His successor found himself obliged to raise the tax rate an additional $13, and decided not to face the voters in the 1961 elections. So long as higher taxes are not at issue, campaigning for office in Malden resembles campaigning in Lynn and Waltham—appealing to friends and neighbors on a platform of better streets, police protection, and so on. The composition of the 1964-65 city council reflected the lower-middle-class orientation of Malden politics—five small businessmen, two hourly employees, an advertising salesman, a schoolteacher, a newspaperman, and a statehouse employee. One councilor, who used his store as a center for ward politics, explained his interest in city politics in these simple terms: "I like to help people; politics is only good for what you can do for people."

In 1965, the Malden Police Department consisted of 120 men

and officers. The top salary for patrolmen was $6,500, $200 higher than the top pay in Lynn and $500 higher than the top salary in Waltham. The Malden police chief received a salary of $10,000. Unlike the Lynn and Waltham police chiefs, the chief in Malden takes orders from a police commissioner, who is appointed by the mayor and receives a salary of $1,500 per year. It is the police commissioner rather than the chief who prepares the annual budget, makes appointments, and assigns men to positions within the department. Since the commissioner has a three-year term of office, a Malden mayor may frequently have to work with a police commissioner not of his own choosing.

For Malden, perhaps more than for the other cities we have studied, it is somewhat difficult to separate a discussion of the police department from a discussion of local politics. As in the other cities, elected officials in Malden approve budgets and salary levels, call for police action in particular situations, and so forth. In 1965, for example, following a series of unsolved house-breaks, the mayor ordered all members of the police department to put in four hours of unpaid overtime work per week. (Within several weeks, the burglars were caught, and normal schedules were resumed.)

In addition to these official actions regarding policy and operations, Malden has also seen policemen active in politics and politicians active in police affairs. Present and past mayors and police commissioners mentioned that politicians call them to have friends moved to pleasant assignments within the department. The present mayor mentioned that Malden has had a long tradition of jumping top-ranked men on civil-service examination lists, although only one such jumping (when the applicant had a police record) has occurred in recent years. The present chief, John Buckley, was raised to the rank of lieutenant in 1943 when the commissioner skipped the top man, Joseph Henry. In 1944, however, a new commissioner skipped top-ranked Buckley to appoint as chief second-ranked Henry; Buckley had to wait until Henry's retirement in 1960 to move into the chief's office. The police commissioner since 1963 has been John Sheehan, a county court officer and deputy sheriff. His predecessor as commissioner had been active in the campaign of Mayor Donnelly (1960-61) and contributed to the campaign fund of a Republican legislator in 1963.

Several members of the police department have also been interested in local and state politics. Mayor Kelliher and five of the eleven members of the 1964-65 city council had relatives on the police force. During the 1964 senatorial campaign of Edward M. Kennedy, several members of the liquor and vice squad solicited campaign contributions in Malden bars, until the *Evening News* threatened to expose this as a shakedown. Since 1950, Chief Buckley has served as the statehouse lobbyist of the Massachusetts Police Association, a state-wide organization representing all policemen. Chief Buckley was president of the association in 1957 and was honored by 1,500 people, including Governor Volpe, at a testimonial dinner given for him in 1960. A sergeant in the Malden Police Department is secretary of the Massachusetts Police Association.

In 1963, the "political activities" of Chief Buckley—no one was sure whether this meant his attempt to have the outgoing police commissioner reappointed or his statehouse work for the police association—got him into trouble with his superiors. Mayor Kelliher and Commissioner Sheehan ordered Buckley to spend more time at headquarters and less at the statehouse. At one point, Buckley was ordered to sign in and out of headquarters like a college girl in a dormitory. By 1965, however, observers felt that Buckley and Sheehan had come to terms on the lobbying issue; Buckley continues to work for the police association but spends more time in Malden.

There is some evidence that the Malden Police Department takes a rather complacent attitude toward gambling and vice. In 1958, following complaints by housewives that their husbands were squandering their paychecks by placing bets in two Malden bars, the lieutenant in charge of the gambling and vice squad reported that no evidence of gambling could be found at either place; within a few days, the state police raided the two bars and arrested a number of men for bookmaking.[2] In the ensuing district-court trial, the proprietor of one bar testified that the profits from bookmaking were split four ways. The judge's comment, "I wonder where the police came in on this split?" went unanswered.[3] The lieutenant in charge of the vice squad was transferred to the night shift for a few months, but was soon back at his old post. Despite periodic raids by the state police, councilors interviewed in 1965 felt that a number of bookmaking establishments were still in business; they implied that the Malden police knew where they were and yet chose to do nothing about them.

The easy-going attitude of the Malden Police Department toward local gambling extends to the internal operations of the department. New recruits are trained by older men on the force rather than in the formal academies of the state police or FBI. In 1962, Chief Buckley told a visiting British anthropologist that he was trying to run his department like "one big family";[4] two

2. "Board Orders Two Raided Cafes Closed," *Malden Evening News,* March 12, 1959.

3. *Malden Evening News,* February 23, 1959.

4. Michael Banton, *The Policeman in the Community* (London: Tavistock, 1964), p. 79.

years later, Buckley criticized his predecessor for being "a Hitler, a man who doesn't understand other people's problems." Policemen on the force remembered the former chief as a strict disciplinarian; Chief Buckley is regarded by the men as one of their own. To eliminate the animosities caused by assignments based on political influence, appointments since 1960 have been based strictly on civil-service examination lists, and work assignments have been made on the basis of seniority, with the oldest men being given day work.

Chief Buckley's desire to "understand other people's problems" has been shared by recent police commissioners. Commissioner Bateman, a telephone-company official who directed the department between 1960 and 1963, said that he felt that a commissioner should be the public-relations man for the department; at every opportunity, Bateman spoke before church groups, clubs, and PTAs about the department and its problems with crime and delinquency. Commissioner Sheehan, appointed in 1963, also felt it was his job to represent the department before the public; Sheehan has been active in several charitable projects in the city. With the exception of the complaints about gambling mentioned earlier and the normal calls to headquarters to stop traffic violations or vandalism in particular areas, the Malden Police Department is favorably regarded; mayors and councilors thought the force was doing a good job or said they had never heard any complaints about it.

When we look at the traffic-enforcement activities of the Malden Police Department, we note two things—the department is not organized to maximize enforcement efforts, and the attitude of complacency and the emphasis on understanding other people's problems carries over into traffic work, leading the men to write few traffic tickets even when violations have been observed. In

1964, the Malden police ticketed 416 persons,[5] an average of 16.8 persons per thousand motor vehicles and 3.5 persons per officer. These ticketing figures are compared with Lynn and Waltham figures in Table 11. Though total ticketing has increased to a

Table 11. Persons Ticketed in Lynn, Waltham, and Malden, 1964

City	Persons ticketed	Persons per 1,000 motor vehicles	Persons per policeman
Lynn	502	11.9	2.7
Waltham	4,901	158.3	49.0
Malden	416	16.8	3.5

certain extent since John Buckley became chief in 1960, and though the proportion of violators brought into court has increased, ticketing in Malden has remained much lower since 1950—under two chiefs and four commissioners—than ticketing in Waltham (see Table 12).

The traffic department of the Malden police force is run by two lieutenants who formerly had other duties, not by men who had been interested in traffic matters. One lieutenant, who handles the clerical work (seeing to it that ticket forms and accident reports are typed up and the files are kept in order), was the man in charge of the gambling squad at the time of the state police raids mentioned earlier. In his early sixties, he has no great desire to change things. "I could retire now," he noted, "but running the traffic department gives me some place to go in the morning." The other lieutenant, who supervises the men directing traffic and guarding school crossings, is the nephew of Police Commis-

5. Since the Malden Police Department keeps records on the basis of *violations* rather than persons ticketed, this figure of 416 persons ticketed was calculated from ticket-book audit sheets kept by the Registry of Motor Vehicles.

sioner Sheehan. He previously worked on the night shift in the records room. "The captain told me that Jim was very good at clerical work," the commissioner recalled. "There's a lot of paper work to do in traffic, so I knew he'd be perfect for this job."

As in the Lynn and Waltham departments, Malden police officers do not carry Registry ticket books to record traffic violations. Policemen take from the traffic department as many unnumbered forms as they wish to carry; no one keeps track of how

Table 12. Traffic-Law Enforcement in Malden, 1950–1964

Year	Chief	Commis- sioner	Violators given verbal warnings	Violations in court	Court violations per 1,000 motor vehicles
1950	Joseph Henry	McDermod	786	180	10.1
1951	(1950–1959)	(1950–1955)	265	125	6.8
1952			339	265	14.5
1953			346	217	11.2
1954			341	219	11.0
1955			297	195	9.1
1956		Moxham	303	266	12.4
1957		(1956–1959)	375	223	10.1
1958			495	249	11.5
1959			540	304	13.3
1960	John Buckley	Bateman	600	289	12.3
1961	(1960–1964)	(1960–1962)	629	324	13.4
1962			315	623	25.8
1963		Sheehan	305	504	20.4
1964		(1963–1964)	315	462	18.7

Note. The Malden Police Department keeps records on the basis of the number of violations brought into court. The figures in this table use this measure whereas in the text, as in other chapters, figures are given on the basis of number of *persons* given Registry tickets, whether or not these persons are brought into court. Thus the number of court violations in 1964 (462) is greater than the number of persons ticketed (416).

many forms have been issued to each man and no one records how many completed forms have been turned in by each man. Clerks in the traffic department type up Registry tickets, and the chief decides what recommendation will be made on each one. As in Lynn, and unlike Waltham, the arresting police officer in Malden must appear in court when a traffic case is first called; he cannot wait until a motorist pleads not guilty.

Interviews with members of the Malden department revealed no incidents of actual harassment of zealous ticket writers (of the "Well, did you ask him *why* he was speeding?" type we saw in Lynn), but several comments indicated that ticket writing was not particularly encouraged:

> A former commissioner: "I always encourage the traffic men to be courteous to motor violators. I think diplomacy buys more than tough talk. I don't like to get reports of discourtesy."
>
> A lieutenant in the traffic department: "I don't care how many tickets the men bring in. I'd rather see people get accustomed to stopping at stop signs than to book them. Some 'active' young men write too many tickets and bring in motorists who weren't going very much over the speed limit. People can speed; it's only when their driving is *erratic* that we write tickets."
>
> A sergeant in the traffic department: "No one is pushed to write tickets. Sometimes, though, you'll find an 'eager beaver' that likes to write lots of tickets."

This lack of interest in traffic work is reflected in the assignment of men. As in Lynn, most officers are told to look for traffic violations when they are not tied up with other duties. Although two men are assigned to traffic-violation work, they only look for violations when they are not guarding school crossings, investigating accidents, or answering miscellaneous "traffic" calls such as "Check for an abandoned car on Ferry Street" or "There is a car blocking traffic on Glenwood Avenue." In the first five months of 1965, these two men wrote 133 tickets, or 35 percent of the 375 tickets written by the force during this period. The two traffic "specialists" in Malden thus work under handicaps (their other "traffic" duties) not found in Waltham, but it is clear that they also have a different conception of enforcement than their counterparts in Waltham. First, whereas the Waltham enforcement men select certain high-violation sites (on the basis of citizen complaints and police observations) and simply wait there to catch violators, the Malden men tend to drive randomly around the city and take whatever comes their way. More important, these men have adopted an attitude toward traffic violations which is as complacent as that of the commissioner quoted earlier. The following statement, made to me by one of the traffic men as we were sitting in a patrol car near an intersection ("This is one of the worst intersections in the city—lots of accidents"), speaks for itself.

> Did you see the car going through that stop sign? It was going 5, maybe 10 m.p.h. You could book 500 cars per day at 5 m.p.h. It's partly those automatic transmissions cars have today—it's pretty hard to come to a full stop. We've all gotten into the habit of coasting through stop signs. We only book them if they go through stop signs at 15 m.p.h. or more.

In Malden, then, we see many of the attitudes that were prevalent in the Lynn Police Department. With the exception of two men, no one is specifically assigned to traffic work. No one is particularly expected to write tickets, and no one keeps track of how many tickets are written by each man. Official policies do not encourage ticket writing and the emphasis placed upon courtesy may discourage it; the penalties for discourtesy are more likely to be applied by superior officers than any possible rewards for vigorous enforcement work. Finally, though two men have been denominated enforcement men by the chief, they are also given other duties to perform so that ticket writing is not the full measure of their day's work. Their personal attitude toward violations —don't write a ticket unless it is a flagrant violation—is in accord with the views stated by their superiors.

5 / Cambridge: Changing Organizational Incentives

"Policemen write as many traffic tickets as you encourage them to write."

—Cambridge Police Chief Daniel J. Brennan

A Cambridge bank once distributed a film entitled "Cambridge—The Unknown City." A more accurate title might have been "The Two Faces of Cambridge." One face is the known face—the buildings, faculties, and students of Harvard and MIT, and the stately mansions of the Brattle Street area of the city. The unknown face of Cambridge is that of its large working-class population and the three-decker houses that fill North and East Cambridge.[1]

When we try to fit Cambridge into the typology developed in my introduction, we discover at least three different forces active in Cambridge politics, each with its own view of the proper role of local government. One, the Cambridge Civic Association, recruits most of its 3,500 members from the Harvard and MIT communities and the Brattle Street area. In the 1963 elections for the city council, the six CCA candidates received 12,928, or 40 percent, of the votes cast; four CCA endorsees were elected to the nine-man council. The CCA (although not all of its endorsed

1. Information on Cambridge's population and economy is from Massachusetts Department of Commerce, Division of Research, *Monograph No. 57: City of Cambridge* (1964).

candidates) has generally pushed for economic growth—such as urban-renewal projects and new highways that will make the city attractive to industrial and research concerns; particularly it is felt that Cambridge should be assisted in competing with the Route 128 area north and west of Boston for this type of development. Since basic municipal services have already been provided, promotion of economic growth requires "efficient management" of the city's affairs (such as support of the manager form of government). The CCA has also demanded such "amenities" as increased facilities for schools, recreation, and mental health.

The second major group active in Cambridge politics, known as the "independents," advocates the low-tax, low-service caretaker philosophy that we found in Lynn and Malden. Representing the working-class residents of North and East Cambridge, this faction has generally sought to keep the tax rate down at any price (in fact, over the last twenty years, Cambridge taxes have risen less than those in neighboring cities), to avoid highway or renewal projects that might displace families (the projects completed in Cambridge, it might be noted, have displaced almost as many businesses as families), and generally to work within the existing consensus form of government (that is, not bringing outside professionals into the city bureaucracy).

Since the independents, like the CCA, generally only win two or three seats on the city council, the balance of power in Cambridge politics is usually held by a third group, which has been able to capture the mayor's and city manager's positions by mediating between the CCA and the independents. Although council debates on most municipal issues have been highlighted by acrimonious exchanges between the two extreme groups, the policies actually adopted are generally those of the arbiter group. An editorial in the Cambridge newspaper summarized the history of the council-manager plan: "The kind of city government we have enjoyed in recent years has been 'compromise government' with neither the Independents nor the CCA in full control."[2] The offices of mayor and city manager have almost always been filled by men tolerable to both extreme groups but completely satisfactory to neither. The mayor from 1960 to 1965 was an Irish-American Democrat whose father was a Cambridge policeman; he was also a graduate of Harvard College and Harvard Law School. The city manager from 1951 until 1965 was an Irish-American native of Cambridge who used to teach in the Cambridge school system; he held a B.S. from Harvard and a Ph.D. in romance philology from Boston College. In 1966, the council appointed as city manager an Italian-American native of the city who holds degrees from Harvard College and Harvard Law School.

For the last ten years, the Cambridge Police Department has varied in size between 225 and 235 men and officers. Vacancies at all levels (including the position of chief) are filled by the city manager, but the top name on the civil-service lists is always taken. Cambridge tries to keep its police salaries higher than in any other city in the state; the top pay for patrolmen in 1965 was $6,958—forty cents more, several councilors proudly noted, than the top salary for the Metropolitan District Police.

The Cambridge police chief from 1951 to 1957 was Patrick F. "Buster" Ready. Outsiders thought of Ready as a rough, tough cop, the kind we might picture wading into a fight and knocking a few heads together. It is reported that when he got angry with his men, he lost his temper and screamed at them. Oldtimers on the Cambridge force remember his ability to "chew out" his men

2. Editorial in *Cambridge Chronicle,* July 1, 1965.

—on their own terms and in their own language. Having vented his wrath, however, the chief bore no grudges and was soon back on good terms with the erstwhile miscreant. He had spent most of his police years on the detective squad, and critics claimed he thought little of any aspect of police life other than detective work.

When Chief Ready retired in 1957, a civil-service examination was held. (A captain who was about to retire was named interim chief.) The top man on the examination list was Daniel Brennan, a Cambridge native who had been on the force since 1930. As an officer, he had served in every division of the force; in 1958, he had charge of training and supervising the auxiliary police force. Brennan had been sent to the FBI National Academy in Washington as a sergeant. Comparing him with Ready, everyone thought of Brennan as a "book" cop, one who did things according to the rules.

Outsiders see Dan Brennan as a quiet, courteous man—a nonsmoking, nondrinking gentleman. The men on the Cambridge force quickly discovered that he was not going to be very "gentlemanly" in his conduct of the department. First, there were minor inconveniences—he demanded, for example, that the image of the force be improved through attention to neatness and courtesy toward the public; any officer seen smoking in public or visiting a bar while on duty would be immediately reprimanded. (Brennan told of a priest who walked into his office holding a speeding ticket he had received while driving in "civilian" clothes. "I'm sorry, father," he said, "we don't like to bother the clergy. Why didn't you tell the officer who you were?" "Oh," the priest replied, "the officer was so polite to me that I was sure I wasn't going to get a ticket.")

Next Brennan undertook to change the force by revamping its

training programs. Like other Massachusetts cities with populations over 100,000, Cambridge has its own police academy. Brennan put a lieutenant with whom he had worked closely in charge
of the academy, went out of his way to bring in instructors from
the Red Cross, the courts, the FBI, and the Registry of Motor
Vehicles, and even offered to train new recruits from neighboring
cities free of charge. Brennan has subjected men at all levels to a
barrage of in-service training programs. Once every three years,
every man receives first-aid training; there are also annual training sessions in weaponry and marksmanship. Officers have been
sent to outside seminars on Search and Seizure Law, Traffic-En-
gineering Problems, Supervision of Police Personnel, and Medico-
Legal Problems of Murder and Suicide.

To the men, these new policies were relatively painless. "If he
wants us to go to school, we'll go to school," one reflected. A
third change initiated by Brennan did not turn out to be so pleasant: he took a number of steps to find out exactly what each man
on the force was doing. If a man called in sick too often, Brennan would send a doctor to his home to check on the illness. To
counteract any inclination that route patrolmen might have to
pretend to be calling headquarters from call box A when in fact
they were calling from a more accessible box or from home,
Brennan installed a device that recorded exactly when and from
which box each man was calling. One dispatcher who regularly
reported receiving calls that in fact were nonexistent or from a
different box was recently given punishment (unpaid) duty of
twenty-five hours; a patrolman who liked to go home after his last
required call (forty-five minutes before the end of the shift) was
assigned one hundred hours of punishment work.

Finally, Brennan instituted a system of "daily work reports."
At the end of his tour of duty, each policeman fills out a form

stating his day's assignments, any arrests made, moving and parking violation tickets written, and so on. The commanding officer of each division reviews these reports daily, and Brennan gets a monthly summary for each man. His critics charge that he is thereby imposing a quota of tickets on each man; Brennan feels that he is kept too busy worrying about the men who write *no* tickets in a month to care whether other men write ten tickets or a hundred.

Brennan's increased supervision of his men caused fairly widespread resentment; a few men quit, and others complained to their friends on the city council. But since civil-service rules permit a chief to transfer men to different posts and to assign punishment duties, there was no other way in which to object to these new rules. Brennan's position has been less secure on two other policies, ones that have shaken the department over the last few years. The first concerns a departmental rule that all members of the force must be residents of Cambridge. Civil-service rules provide only that applicants for entrance examinations must have resided within the city for six months; they say nothing about continuing to live there. The Cambridge force has had a continued-residence rule for at least forty years. It became a problem only after World War II, when Cambridge property values began rising rapidly. The rule was relaxed and returning veterans were the first to move beyond city limits; by 1965, 35 of the 235 men on the force lived outside Cambridge. Some lived as far as forty miles away.

Brennan's position was difficult—many of the nonresidents were highly trusted superior officers. He felt, however, that resident policemen were more effective than nonresidents because they had greater opportunities to prevent crime and because they could get closer to the community. But to demand that nonresidents move back or face dismissal charges might lead to his being left with almost no supervisory officers. He tried two less drastic measures. First, in 1961, he announced that nonresidents would no longer be eligible for pay details—the off-duty assignments such as weddings, funerals, or department-store sales that can add $10 or $20 to a patrolman's weekly paycheck. Second, he refused to promote nonresidents. An examination for several captains' positions was held in April 1964; the first man on the list was a resident, the second through fifth men were nonresidents. He immediately promoted the first man, who was already serving as court prosecutor. One year later, when my study was made, Brennan was still "sitting" on the other promotions, although several of the men were doing a captain's work at lieutenant's pay. He also refused to skip the nonresidents, even though the next resident on the list (in sixth position) was commanding the entire uniformed division. He did not dismiss the nonresidents from the force—when a man tells him that he will be moving from Cambridge, Brennan simply informs him that he will be forfeiting his promotion and pay-detail privileges.

Several attempts to press Brennan on the residency issue failed. Several councilmen tried to pass an ordinance repealing the department rule. The city manager intervened, declaring that it was purely a matter of administration and therefore beyond the jurisdiction of the council. The manager asked Brennan if he wanted to change the rule; when Brennan said no, the manager accepted his decision. Another councilor, related by marriage to the sixth man on the captains' list (a Cambridge resident), introduced a resolution affirming the department's rule so that Brennan would be forced to skip the nonresidents; the ordinance failed to pass.

A second *cause célèbre* on the Cambridge police scene concerns policemen in politics. In 1963, a Cambridge detective ran for the city council and finished tenth in the nine-man election. Quoting Oliver Wendell Holmes' famous statement that "every man has a right to run for public office but no man has a right to be a policeman," Chief Brennan "busted" the detective, transferring him to traffic duty "for the good of the department." Although the detective had violated the state corrupt-practices act by soliciting campaign contributions, Brennan felt that the reassignment was adequate punishment. In 1964, a patrolman ran unsuccessfully for the legislature; since his campaign was financed entirely from his own funds, Brennan did not take disciplinary action, but issued a department rule forbidding members of the force to campaign for or hold public office. In a special election in May 1965, however, this patrolman won a seat in the legislature. Brennan denied his request for a leave of absence and transferred him to the day shift, when most legislative sessions were held. Brennan's refusal to grant the leave of absence led to a full-scale council hearing, with the "independent" councilors calling the chief a "phony" and a "dictator." The Cambridge Civic Association came out in support of Brennan. In a classic statement of the philosophy of the city-manager form of government, the city manager backed up Brennan, declaring that the council had no right to interfere in the administration of city departments.[3] A compromise was finally reached whereby Brennan agreed to grant the patrolman a leave of absence, and the patrolman agreed to resign from the force if he was re-elected to the legislature in 1966.

3. "Lombardi's Leave Issue Hangs Fire till Next Monday," *Cambridge Chronicle,* June 10, 1965; "Lombardi Action Is Backed," *Boston Herald,* June 10, 1965; letter from Cambridge City Manager John J. Curry to the Cambridge City Council, *Cambridge Chronicle,* June 17, 1965.

While working to upgrade his department, Dan Brennan has jealously guarded his force against outside "interference," ignoring any council requests he feels to intrude upon the area of administration. The council, for example, regularly passes "orders" to the chief to crack down on speeding on certain streets; the chief may tell one of his motorcycle men to check the streets occasionally. When a local judge declared that Harvard Square was "full of dope peddlers," several councilors demanded that Brennan set up a special narcotics squad; Brennan felt that his regular vice squad was perfectly competent to handle any local narcotics trade and he ignored the councilmen. Early in 1965, following a series of (unheeded) council orders to put more foot patrolmen into certain neighborhoods, the council passed a resolution to increase the size of the force from 235 to 250. Asked about the move, Brennan chuckled: "It's an election year, you know, and citizens have been calling the councilors to ask for more 'protection.' I don't need any more men, so I'm not going to hire them."

In a few cases, however, Brennan has modified some of his policies in the face of intense opposition. It will be recalled that he has refused to skip nonresidents on promotion lists or to dismiss men seeking to move out of Cambridge. Another policy that might be labeled unprofessional stems not from political pressures or from a desire not to disrupt his department, but rather from a feeling of kinship with other police chiefs in the state. For several years, Brennan has served as the statehouse lobbyist for the Massachusetts Chiefs of Police Association. Although he has allowed his men to carry the Registry violation books, he has refused to counter the association's opposition to a bill requiring distribution of books to the men.

A final policy, of questionable legality, concerns teenagers. At night, a number of teenagers from neighboring cities come into Cambridge to stare at the Harvard hippies or simply "to see what's going on." One two-block area near Harvard Square came to resemble, in Brennan's eyes, a parade ground, with cars full of teenagers slowly circling past student hangouts. Brennan responded to the teenagers by directing his men to take the license numbers of all cars with teenage drivers in the Harvard Square area. Brennan then sent letters to the registered owners of these cars, requesting them to bring the person who was driving this car in Harvard Square on such-and-such a night to Cambridge police headquarters. Writing about a hundred letters, Brennan said, led to a quick cleaning up of the Harvard Square situation. In all but a few cases, the boy's father would call in and say, "I had no idea my son was hanging around Harvard Square. He won't be there again." Brennan's supporters viewed the letter-writing campaign as good police work. A lawyer might reply that unless the teenagers were violating loitering or public-nuisance ordinances, they had every right to be in Harvard Square.

Within the Cambridge Police Department, both the traffic division and the uniformed division (which contains all men not assigned to traffic, detective, or juvenile work) are involved in enforcing traffic laws. The traffic division (28 patrolmen, 4 sergeants, and a lieutenant) handles both traffic direction and traffic enforcement; each traffic-division patrolman spends about three hours a day on enforcement—tagging parked cars and stopping moving violators. The traffic division also has three bike men— patrolmen who, during good weather, patrol the city on motorcycles. All members of the uniformed division, both men walking a beat and men riding in cruisers, are also under orders to enforce parking and traffic laws; at times, one cruiser will be equipped with a radar machine to assist the bike men in "selective" enforcement work. If the orders to the Cambridge uniformed men to enforce traffic laws while performing other duties remind us of the Lynn situation, in which "all men are on traffic" meant that "no men are on traffic," a major difference between the Lynn department and the Cambridge department will be restated— Cambridge Chief Brennan checks the work reports of *every* man to see how many parking and moving-violation tickets have been written in a month, and he reprimands those who produce few or no tickets. Production of traffic tickets is a requirement that Brennan applies to every patrolman on the force, whether in the traffic or the uniformed division.

The system for processing traffic tickets is roughly this: only the three bike men and a few cruiser officers carry Registry ticket books. The other men use numbered ticket forms, printed by the department, which have spaces for the information necessary to complete the Registry form. At the end of his tour of duty, after filling out his daily work report, each officer turns in the day's parking tickets and department or Registry forms for moving violations to his commanding officer—the lieutenant in charge of the traffic division or the captain in charge of the uniformed division. After the violations initially recorded on department forms are transferred to Registry forms, all violation slips are placed on the chief's desk. The arresting officers seldom make suggestions about ticket recommendations; the final recommendation on each ticket is made personally by the chief. The violation slip then goes to the records room, where necessary papers (letters to the Registry, applications for complaints, and such) are filled out. Like the Waltham court, the Cambridge district court only asks the arresting officer in a traffic case to appear in court after a defendant has pleaded not guilty; so court appearances are not a major problem for Brennan.

Table 13 compares the issuance of moving-violation tickets under former Chief Ready and under Dan Brennan. The 1964 moving-violation tickets amounted to an average of 23.7 tickets

Table 13. Ticketing in Cambridge, 1951–1964

Chief	Year	Moving: violation tickets	Tickets per 1,000 motor vehicles
Ready	1951	1,800	55.1
(11/51–11/57)	1952	955	29.1
	1953	n.a.	n.a.
	1954	165	5.3
	1955	173	4.8
	1956	732	21.0
Acting Chief	1957	480	13.6
(11/57–7/58)	1958	2,383	68.9
Brennan	1959	4,569	130.7
(7/58 to 1967)	1960	4,432	133.8
	1961	6,604	189.0
	1962	3,639	98.0
	1963	7,381	190.2
	1964	5,457	143.0

per member of the force and 143.0 tickets per thousand motor vehicles. These figures compare with figures from the three cities studied earlier (correcting for the fact that the first three cities used separate tickets to record each violation by a single motorist), as seen in Table 14.

Who wrote the Cambridge tickets in 1964? The three men on motorcycles wrote 1,175, 1,100, and 800 tickets, or a total of 3,075 of the 5,457 tickets written by the Cambridge force. The

Table 14. Persons Ticketed by Four Police Forces, 1964

City	Persons ticketed	Persons per policeman	Persons per 1,000 motor vehicles
Lynn	502	2.7	11.9
Waltham	4901	49.0	158.3
Malden	416	3.5	16.8
Cambridge	5457	23.7	143.0

remaining tickets were fairly well spread throughout the force; since few officers beside the bike men had their own Registry ticket books, it was difficult to determine how other tickets were divided between the traffic and the uniformed divisions.

During Brennan's years in office, a fairly uniform percentage of Cambridge tickets—between 20 percent and 30 percent—have been marked warnings. But Brennan has varied between Registry and court recommendations when he feels that action should be taken against a motorist. Between January 1 and June 1, 1964, no minor violation (speeding, failing to slow down at an intersection, running a stop sign, and such) was marked for court action unless the violator also tried to get away. Most were given Registry recommendations; the rest were given warnings. After June 1, court recommendations increased, so that for the first nine months of the year, using a one-in-four sample, the recommendations on these minor violations were:

Warning	231	25.5%
Registry	560	61.9
Court	114	12.6
	905	100.0%

This pattern of moderate use of court action, with a basic reliance on the Registry, continued until the end of January 1965. At that point, the relative use of court and Registry suddenly switched. For the first ten weeks in 1965, the recommendations made on minor violations were:

Warning	158	30.4%
Registry	108	20.8
Court	254	48.8
	520	100.0%

The 1964 reliance on Registry action did not, however, extend to the more serious offenses; persons found driving under the influence, driving an unregistered motor vehicle, or driving while their licenses were suspended were just as likely to be brought into court by the Cambridge police as by other police forces.

When asked about these variations, Chief Brennan said that they are based upon circumstances unrelated to the charactor of a violation. Although he would like to send all violations meriting punishment to court, he feels that the Cambridge court is physically unable to process all of the tickets written by the four police forces (three city departments and the Metropolitan District Police) working within the court district. In 1964, Arlington, Belmont, and Cambridge police ticketed 6,823 motorists for minor violations; only 1,180 tickets were marked for court action. It seems that, when the court staff has more work than it can handle, traffic complaints are pushed to one side. At one point, in 1960, Brennan discovered that the court had accumulated 1,000 Cambridge tickets without issuing any summonses. For a few months, Brennan hired a woman on police-department funds to assist the court clerks; he then decided that staffing the court was up to the county and discharged the woman. Since then, Brennan's policy has been to send to court as many cases as the court can process quickly—by sending out a summons within two to three weeks after the violation occurs.

However, Brennan has discovered an unpleasant side effect to this policy of gearing ticket recommendations to the speed with which the court can process them. In the spring of 1964, when he was following a policy of sending all minor violations to the Registry, Brennan was told by one of his traffic men that the word was getting around that Cambridge motorists were not being taken into court. According to Brennan, there is a grapevine operating through which truckers, bus drivers, cab drivers, and especially Harvard and MIT students learn when the Cambridge police are cracking down and when they are taking drivers into court. Whether this grapevine exists or not, Brennan thinks that it does, and so in June 1964 and again early in 1965, he increased the percentage of court recommendations, "mixing them up," as he put it, "so that they won't know what we are going to do."

The year 1958, when Dan Brennan became chief, marked a turning point in Cambridge traffic-law enforcement. In trying to understand the reasons behind the tenfold increase in the writing of moving-violation tickets, we might first look to see whether any conditions outside the police department could have led to an increased interest in traffic enforcement. One such condition might be a change in the volume of traffic in the city. As in all parts of the United States, Cambridge has seen a per capita increase in automobile ownership since World War II, reinforced by an influx of student-owned cars. Apart from students, however, the population of Cambridge has been steadily declining (by 10.8 percent between 1950 and 1960); thus the absolute number of automobiles has probably not risen as fast in Cambridge as in other parts of the state or nation.

A second measure of the traffic problem in a city might be the number of traffic accidents. Table 15 shows the property-damage, personal-injury, and fatal accidents occurring in Cambridge in the years 1950–1964, together with the number of moving-violation tickets written. Two things should be noted about these accident figures. First, there was no change in accident experience at or just before the time Brennan became chief, which might suggest that he was reacting to an "alarming" increase in accidents. The second point, however, is that Cambridge has had a higher number of traffic accidents than any other city of its size in the state. For the period between 1961 and 1963, Cambridge

Table 15. Cambridge Traffic Accidents and Traffic Tickets, 1950–1964

Year	Property-damage accidents[a]	Personal injury accidents	Fatal accidents	Moving-violation tickets
1950	—	1,402	14	n.a.
1951	—	1,364	8	1,800
1952	—	1,130	6	955
1953	—	1,326	4	n.a.
1954	—	1,479	2	165
1955	—	1,516	2	173
1956	—	1,632	9	732
1957	270	1,641	3	480
1958	288	1,605	8	2,383
1959	276	1,686	6	4,569
1960	302	1,740	7	4,432
1961	306	1,639	7	6,604
1962	364	1,664	7	3,639
1963	326	1,945	7	7,381
1964	475	2,065	9	5,457

Source. Massachusetts Registry of Motor Vehicles, "Motor Vehicle Traffic Accidents, Injuries, and Deaths," issued annually.

[a] Until 1954, the Registry did not collect information on property-damage accidents. From 1954 until June 1956, it collected reports from all accidents involving damage of more than $100. Since June, 1956, it has collected information only on accidents involving property damage of more than $200.

had an average of 54.7 traffic accidents (of all types) per thousand registered motor vehicles; the three cities closest to it in size had 38.7, 28.8, and 38.2 accidents per thousand motor vehicles. This can be partially attributed to the fact that Cambridge is a corridor city through which much traffic between Boston and the northern suburbs must pass; other cities have a higher proportion of local traffic.

The general relation between traffic accidents and intensity of law enforcement will be considered later. At this point, it will be suggested only that Cambridge's high accident rate would make it likely that its police department would be more concerned with traffic than would police in cities with lower accident rates. If this is true, we are still left with the problem of explaining the lack of interest in traffic enforcement demonstrated by the department under former Chief Ready, when the accident rate was much the same as it was in the Brennan period. In other words, the accident figures do not tell us why one chief responded to a high accident rate by writing 5,000 tickets while a former chief responded to the same accident rate by writing one tenth as many. It might also be noted that the change in enforcement policy in Cambridge has had no noticeable effect on the accident rate.

A second explanation for Brennan's interest in writing traffic tickets is offered by a few local politicians, who felt that Brennan was being overzealous about traffic (he was harassing "innocent" motorists). They claim that Brennan had increased his enforcement activities against both parking and moving violators to satisfy the city manager's hunger for nontax-based revenues.[4] These critics argue that while the $217,406 the city of Cambridge

4. All parking-meter receipts and fines go to the city. Fines for moving violations go to the city if a *city* ordinance (one-way street, stop sign, no

received from meter violations in 1964 was equal only to 1.16 percent of the city's 1965 budget, it provided a fund that the city manager could use to more than cover the cost of his traffic department ($143,000 in 1965) or to provide other programs without raising the tax rate.

At first glance, this explanation is tempting. After 1959, Brennan's first full year as chief, the police department's budget increased from $1.5 million to $2.1 million in 1965; patrolmen's salaries have increased from $4,700 to $6,958; the chief's salary has risen from $8,300 to $12,450. It seems clear, the proponents of the "increase the city's revenues" theory insist, that the city manager is paying off Brennan for cracking down on traffic violators. Unfortunately, three facts weaken this "payoff" theory. First, police-salary increases are voted by the council and the manager must provide for them in his budget. Second, police-salary increases (accounting for most of the budget increases) have coincided with similar increases in the salaries of *all* city employees; if anyone was "bribing" Brennan, he was doing it while raising all other salaries as well. Third, Chief Ready, uninterested in enforcing traffic and parking laws and therefore less active in enriching the city treasury, was just as successful as Brennan in winning increases from the same city manager. Ready's budget rose from $1 million in 1952 to $1.4 million in 1958; patrolmen's salaries rose from $3,660 to $4,700; and the chief's salary rose from $6,500 to $8,000. Finally, even if this explanation were valid for Cambridge, it would still leave unexplained the *lack* of ticketing in other cities in the state, each of which is presumably just as much interested in revenue.

---

left turn, and such) is violated; fines for the violation of *state* law (improper speed, driving under the influence, driving to endanger) go to the counties.

What then is left of the "increase city revenues" explanation for Brennan's interest in traffic enforcement? It is obvious that the city manager is not unhappy that he has had this extra money to work with; he also said that he liked the way Brennan was running the force, although he did not mention the revenues resulting from it. What is missing from the argument is a connecting link—that since the manager would like as much revenue as possible, he would pressure the chief in some way to adopt a policy (strict enforcement) to support such a goal. It is certainly true that a manager can influence a department head by ways other than cutting his budget; what seems questionable is that he would regularly increase the budget of a department head whose policies he theoretically disliked. Thus we can only say that, though the manager liked the monetary results of Brennan's policy, he did not attempt budgetary reprisals against Ready for his relatively lax enforcement policies.

These "outside" explanations seem to provide us with little information about why the Brennan police force was different from the Ready police force on matters of traffic enforcement. Only two conclusions seem to remain: first, the change in enforcement policy is basically a matter of change in the personality, interests, and attitudes of the chief; second, the political make-up of Cambridge is such that a city department head can with impunity align himself with whatever faction and group of policies he chooses.

On the first point, everyone interviewed attributed the strict enforcement policy after 1958 to the influence of Brennan on his force rather than to any changing conditions in the city. Several pro-Brennan councilors said, "Brennan is making his men do a good day's work. If there is a law on the books, he wants it enforced." One anti-Brennan councilor, though disliking the effects, concurred on the cause: "Brennan is always after the bike men to write more and more tickets." Patrolmen on the force attribute the increase in tickets directly to the change at the top, sensing that any pressure put on them by intermediate officers (sergeants, lieutenants, and captains) only reflects the demands made by Brennan. As one traffic patrolman bitterly said, "Brennan has set himself up as the kingpin—he's the only boss in this outfit, and you don't argue with him. If he says that white car over there is black, believe me, it's black." Another traffic man, who personally enjoyed writing traffic tickets, said that Brennan was giving the bike men more time to work on enforcement, freeing them from other police duties. The change in organizational norms, it might be noted, has been accomplished without any change in personnel—the three bike men who wrote 3,975 tickets for Brennan in 1964 were the same men who were riding motorcycles for Ready in 1955, when the entire force wrote only 173 tickets. Earlier, when discussing Brennan's interest in on-the-job training programs, I noted an attitude among the men of "If he wants us to go to school, we'll go to school." Since the bike men prefer their traffic work to walking a beat, they seem to have said to themselves, without noticeable grumbling, "If he wants us to write tickets, we'll write tickets."

The second point brings up a question of the relation between the character of a city, however defined, and the traffic-enforcement policies of its police force. In Cambridge, as mentioned earlier, there are three faces of the city—the good government, upper-middle-class character of Brattle Street, the universities, and the Cambridge Civic Association; the "friends and neighbors," lower-middle-class character of North and East Cambridge; and the arbiter character of the group that, combining North and East Cambridge Irish-Catholic ancestry with ties to the universities, has produced a faction in city politics capable of mediating between the extremes, seizing the pivotal mayor's and city manager's positions.

To a great extent, Cambridge police chiefs may be viewed as occupying a position similar to that of the city manager. Chief Ready tended toward the East Cambridge side of "center," while staying on sufficiently cordial terms with the center to get regular budget and pay raises. Brennan has taken his force to the opposite side of center, alienating several East Cambridge councilors while not quite satisfying the Brattle Streeters. The Brattle Street faction has never been able to dismiss completely the nonresidents and policeman-politicians on the force. Their general view might be summed up in the statement on one CCA member —"Dan Brennan is a well-intentioned man without very much imagination." But when, in May 1965, three anti-CCA councilors supported a move to create a position of police commissioner— a noncivil-service appointee who would stand over the police chief—the four CCA councilors joined two center men to defeat the proposal.[5]

Given this tripartite character of Cambridge politics, and given the fact that the city manager, because of the civil-service system and the council's control over police salaries, cannot do too much to put pressure on his police chief even if he wanted to, it would seem that a Cambridge police chief can do almost anything he likes with his force—making it more professional, as Brennan chose to do, or adopting a lenient attitude, as Ready did. The budget figures presented earlier suggest that, unless a chief alienates the center of Cambridge politics, he will not encounter many difficulties.

5. "City Council Covers Whole Waterfront," *Cambridge Chronicle,* May 20, 1965.

Part II / Policymaking in Traffic-Law Enforcement

6 / The Political Context: Public Pressures on the Police

The case studies presented in Part One showed that those police forces which displayed a high level of ticketing combined a specialized function of traffic-law enforcement with a definite policy on the part of superior officers that violators should be ticketed rather than let off with verbal warnings. Low-ticketing forces felt that traffic was a less important police function and that most violators should be ignored or given a verbal warning. To understand the context in which police departments formulate these policies regarding traffic-law enforcement, we can now ask more generally what the enforcement of traffic laws means to police departments. Who cares whether the police chief pushes ticket writing or encourages his men in other directions, whether to concentrate on other aspects of police work (preventing or solving robberies, helping pedestrians across the street) or to take a nonticketing attitude toward traffic violations (either ignoring violations entirely or giving a courteous warning to persons stopped)? What difference will it make whether the patrolman writes tickets or fails to see violations? In the next chapter we shall consider the extent to which traffic policies can be predicted from court, accident, or demographic data from the communities in which the police work. In the last chapter we shall look at internal relations within police departments—the organizational context of traffic-law enforcement. Here we shall consider traffic policies in terms of relations between police departments and outside agencies—the general public, other police departments, safety organizations, and elected officials.

To begin with, is police policymaking in traffic-law enforcement an area in which there is active citizen participation? Or is it an area of low interest and involvement? The likelihood that members of a community care about traffic-enforcement policies might be bolstered by the so-called objective importance of these policies. With the possible exception of the schoolteacher, the traffic policeman is probably the municipal employee with whom the average citizen has the greatest personal contact. In addition, police work accounts for a significant portion of the municipal budget—the mean percent of general expenditures devoted to police work in the 508 cities studied was 12 percent.[1] (Although there is no evidence that a strict enforcement policy would be either more or less expensive than a lenient policy, the size of the police budget might be expected to attract at least some public interest.) Finally, police enforcement policies would seem to be important to the community because of the commonly accepted view that strict enforcement will promote traffic safety and thus reduce insurance rates.[2]

Although these factors would suggest that the residents of a community *should* care about traffic policies, two facts make it unlikely that the police would receive a clear popular mandate regarding the extent or direction that traffic enforcement should take. First, enforcement *policies* (as opposed to individual actions) tend to be completely unknown or irrelevant to most mem-

1. Data on police expenditures are from the 1962 Census of Governments.
2. See, e.g., O. W. Wilson, *Police Administration*, 2nd ed. (New York: McGraw-Hill, 1963), ch. 17, "Traffic Administration."

bers of the community. Most traffic violations do not involve a "victim" who would have a personal interest in police action. Furthermore, since most police officials try to foster a public impression that *all* violations will be punished, they conceal any department policies that would lead to ignoring one class of crime (such as minor traffic violation), or to concentrating upon violations in one part of the city, or to setting an official tolerance level (such as specifying that tickets will only be written when the motorist exceeds the speed limit by 15 m.p.h.).[3] Thus, even if they were interested in police ticketing policies, it would be almost impossible for most citizens to discover what they were.

A second fact weakening the impact of any popular mandate is the ambivalence of public attitudes toward traffic laws—a vague desire for safety combined with a personal desire not to get a ticket. There is probably a community consensus that serious violations—driving under the influence of alcohol, reckless driving, and soon—should be prosecuted as vigorously as crimes of violence or crimes against property. At the opposite extreme, there is probably also a feeling that traffic officers should display some degree of leniency; if a policeman suddenly becomes a "ticketing fool"—ticketing old ladies going one mile over the speed limit or motorists racing to the hospital—the chief will be expected to "sit on him" or "bury him" in some location where he will not antagonize the public.

Between these two extremes, however, police chiefs feel rela-

3. Wayne R. LaFave, *Arrest: The Decision To Take a Suspect into Custody* (Boston: Little, Brown, 1965), pp. 153–157; Joseph Goldstein, "Police Discretion Not To Invoke the Criminal Process: Low-Visibility Decisions in the Administration of Justice," *Yale Law Journal*, LXIX (March 1960), 543–594; Herman Goldstein, "Police Discretion: The Ideal versus the Real," *Public Administration Review*, XXIII (September 1963), 140–148.

tively free to handle traffic-law enforcement in any way they choose. There is probably a vague community feeling that traffic safety is a desirable goal, and newspapers will regularly deplore "carnage on the highways," "bad driving habits," and so forth. But in none of the cities studied did newspapers translate an editorial policy supporting traffic safety into a specific demand that the police force adopt an active ticketing program. The only regular newspaper safety campaign in eastern Massachusetts was run by a Boston newspaper. The column, first started in 1956, contains anecdotes about specific bad driving practices or praises policemen or judges who are observed dealing severely with a traffic violator; but it never condemns individuals for a lack of interest in traffic.

The only organizations in Massachusetts interested in traffic safety on a long-term basis are three regional safety councils— the Massachusetts Safety Council (Boston), the Central Massachusetts Safety Council (Worcester), and the Safety Council of Western Massachusetts (Springfield). (There were no safety councils in any of the four cities studied in Part One.) The safety councils are supported by contributions from members, including many of the largest industries in the state. Each council has at least two full-time employees and a clerical staff. The councils conduct public-relations campaigns ("Safe Driving Week," "Accident Prevention Month," and the like), provide safety information to any and all who want it, and lobby to have safety legislation enacted by the legislature and enforced by relevant state and local agencies. In the area of highway safety, the councils have supported the creation of specialized traffic departments or commissions in several cities, the use of chemical tests for intoxication, creation of a learners'-permit system for driver licensing, compulsory installation of seat belts, and the adoption of a no-fix ticketing system.[4]

It is difficult to estimate the influence of the safety councils in this area. A police official in one large midwestern city noted that his city's safety council regularly published a newsletter detailing the traffic-enforcement activities of the local police department; the chief, this official felt, took note of the council's views and pushed his traffic men whenever the council declared that the department was becoming lax. Generally speaking, the Massachusetts safety councils have limited themselves to providing information: telling legislators and judges how reliable chemical intoxication tests are, showing policemen how to investigate accidents, and so forth. From time to time, the executive director of the Massachusetts Safety Council takes members of the Highways and Motor Vehicles Committee of the state legislature on a tour of auto factories in Detroit, a tour that is regarded as one of the major perquisites of membership on this committee. But when safety-council men turn from providing information to demanding that the police act upon it—say by writing more traffic tickets or fixing fewer of them—their influence wanes. The general attitude of the police, according to the safety councils, is "Thank you very much for your information, but please let us run our department our way." Nevertheless, except where matters such as ticket fixing are concerned, relations between police and the safety councils are cordial; happy to get *any* safety enforcement, the council men do not harass the police publicly or complain to city officials.

Whereas police forces are seldom exposed to general public

4. Massachusetts Safety Council, "Legislative Scoreboard through 1964" (1965).

pressure regarding traffic laws, they are frequently bombarded with specific demands. In the largest cities as well as in the smallest towns, citizens call police headquarters (or call elected officials who will relay the message to headquarters) to ask that the police "cut down the speeding in front of my house," or "Tell those kids to stop 'peeling rubber' by the drive-in," or "Watch that stop sign by the grade school." These calls, though received regularly, have an isolated and *ad hoc* character; citizens feel that they have received action if they see a policeman once at the site of these past violations. Although a citizen may see a policeman pull a driver over, he will have no way of knowing how many drivers have been stopped, whether they were given tickets or warnings, or how many of the tickets lead to court action. The pressures to *enforce* traffic laws, then, are limited both as to space and to time—if the citizen who calls can see a policeman at this corner today, he will be satisfied and unconcerned about other corners on other occasions.

What can be said about pressure *against* traffic-law enforcement? A number of police officials have noted that traffic enforcement can jeopardize police–public relations, more than any other phase of police work, diminishing public support for the police when more serious crimes are being investigated.[5] The chief in one small town of 6,000 stated that if he were to engage in an active ticket-writing campaign, the department would suffer when its budget came up at the next town meeting. In two mid-

5. The impact of traffic enforcement on police–public relations is noted in Jerome H. Skolnick, *Justice without Trial: Law Enforcement in a Democratic Society* (New York: John Wiley, 1966), pp. 54–56; T. C. Willett, *Criminal on the Road: A Study of Motoring Offenses and Those Who Commit Them* (London: Tavistock, 1964), ch. 4; and O. W. Wilson, "Police Authority in a Free Society," *Journal of Criminal Law, Criminology, and Police Science*, LIV (June 1964), 175–177.

western cities, chiefs explained that their ticketing rose by 50 percent between 1963 and 1964 simply because 1963 was a local election year and they did not want to make enemies. Most of the Massachusetts chiefs, however, admitted that their enforcement efforts had been hampered—not so much by active pressure against enforcement as by refusals on the part of local officials to provide the men or equipment deemed necessary to operate an adequate program. The chief in Waltham, for example, cited the council's refusal to provide all of the overtime funds he had requested for traffic work. In Malden, the chief had applied without success for funds to purchase a radar machine. Other chiefs failed to secure funds to hire additional men.

Apart from this general limitation—"We'd like to help you, chief, but we're trying to hold the line on taxes"—I found few city officials who were against strict enforcement on general principle. One councilor in Waltham thought that local enforcement standards were too strict, that it was "silly to write a ticket on a stop-sign violation at 11:30 at night." A Cambridge councilor thought that Chief Brennan was harassing his traffic men by demanding too many tickets. Both comments were based on complaints made to the councilors by constituents (by a ticketed motorist in Waltham, by a "harassed" policeman in Cambridge); so it is difficult to say whether the councilors themselves disapproved of the strict policies followed by their police chiefs.

From the point of view of a police chief, then, traffic policymaking must be carried out in a context of sporadic citizen demands that specific actions be taken; pressure for enforcement *in general* is limited to vague, intermittent safety crusades sponsored by newspapers and safety councils. Citizens may remember how quickly their police force apprehends a bank robber or child molester; it is unlikely that a police chief will be praised for a strict enforcement policy or damned for ignoring minor violations. Possibly because involvement in police-department policymaking can impose more political liabilities than assets, many elected officials prefer to avoid *all* comment on police practices. In sum, police officials seldom receive a public mandate by which they can create a traffic-enforcement policy. Rather than rejecting some widely established value system, the police are forced to pick and choose from among many vague and conflicting public values.

Ticket Fixing. One Massachusetts legislator, invited by a local League of Women Voters to discuss the functions of a legislator, startled the ladies by beginning, "The chief function of a legislator is to fix traffic tickets for his constituents." In a state in which most public employees are under the civil-service system, fixing tickets may be one of the few services a legislator can perform for his constituents. One state senator, hearing a safety council official propose a no-fix system, asked incredulously, "Do you really mean that I'm not going to be able to help out friends who get into trouble? There's nothing immoral about fixing minor traffic tickets." Legislators protested an earlier attempt to end fixing on the ground that it would cut down their influence, and they denied a request to increase the size of the state police force after it adopted a no-fix policy.[6]

For the policeman as well as the legislator, requests to fix tickets may well be one of the primary bases of contact with the public. Any motorist, of course, can try to talk his way out of a ticket—"I didn't see the stop sign"; "My speedometer is broken"; "I'm late for work"; and, fairly certain to anger the patrolman,

6. "Legislators Support No-Fix," *Boston Herald,* March 13, 1960; "No-Fix Plan Cuts Accidents," *Boston Herald,* February 28, 1960.

"How dare you stop me? I'm a friend of the governor (bishop, mayor, chief)." But even if a Massachusetts motorist is unable to convince the officer not to write up the offense, there is still a good chance that he can avoid punishment. (The course of action will vary from city to city, depending on whether the policeman carries the Registry ticket books or is recording the facts on a departmental ticket form. In the latter case, the motorist can erase all evidence of the violation if someone in police headquarters rips up the form. If, on the other hand, the arresting officer fills out the Registry tickets on the road—in Cambridge and twenty-seven other cities in the state—the motorist's only hope is to persuade the chief to mark the ticket "warning," since chiefs and policemen fear that someone in the Registry will notice if a Registry form is completely destroyed.)

How does the process of ticket fixing work? Although your ultimate chance for success in getting a ticket fixed (termed by all Massachusetts police officers, "to give consideration") varies from city to city, the list of persons to call does not. Your best bet is to know a member of the police force that stopped you. (If you knew the officer himself, you would not, of course, have received the ticket in the first place.) Other persons to call are: *any* police chief in the state, any policeman in the state, a politician from the city involved, any other politician in the state, and then "friends" of any of these persons. Once you state your case to your contact ("I wasn't going very fast," "I've never had a ticket before," "I need my license to keep my job"), the pattern of communication varies. If your contact does not come from the city in which the ticket is written, he will probably call the chief; someone within the city might have a friend lower down on the force who can take care of it more quietly.

The origins of these lines of communication are lost in antiquity, but their existence is clear. The most effective intercity line of communication is through the home-town police chief. Police chiefs in Massachusetts frequently said that their "constituents" call them regarding tickets received in other towns and that they then call the other chief to ask for consideration for the motorist. The philosophy of all police chiefs seems to be this: the chief should call for his constituent, and the other chief should grant consideration, unless: (1) the Registry ticket has already been written and the recommendation made (if the ticket has been written but the recommendation not yet made, fixing involves a warning rather than destroying or voiding the ticket); (2) the offense is of a serious nature (no chief or politician is willing to involve himself in any situation involving alcohol, accidents, or *dangerous* speeding—"What if the guy later gets involved in an accident or kills somebody? I don't want my name mixed up with his," one city councilor said); or (3) the motorist was rude to the officer. The logic of the last policy is interesting: the chiefs say that they will not intervene for rude motorists because "they are showing disrespect for the law"; it would seem equally likely that they refuse because a rude motorist has got an officer mad, and the cost to the chief of fixing a ticket written by an angered officer is greater than when the officer is less personally interested in the violation or violator. In all three situations, chiefs feel no obligation to their constituents or to other chiefs. Otherwise, Massachusetts chiefs generally seem to assume that consideration will be given; several chiefs said that they would be surprised if another chief did not give consideration in ordinary circumstances.

Several things should be noted about the organization of ticket fixing in Massachusetts. The first is that the general standards used in appraising requests for fixes—the violation is minor, it is a first offense, and the motorist was not rude to the officer—are known and accepted by all of the participants in the system, and few attempt to jeopardize the system by requesting fixes that do not satisfy these standards. A former mayor in one city mentioned that every politician knows at least one person on the force to call, but "if the violation *might* be regarded as 'serious,' the fix has to be cleared with the chief first. If he decides that it is serious, he won't fix it and politicians won't touch it." A councilor added, "I just leave the message with whoever answers the phone at headquarters. If the motorist gave the cop any trouble, or if he was a bad guy (had a prior record), they'll know I don't want to have anything to do with it."

A second interesting aspect of Massachusetts ticket fixing concerns the *quid pro quo* on which the system is based. Even though, according to one probably exaggerated safety-council estimate, half of all traffic tickets written in the state are fixed,[7] it seems that money is not the reason why tickets are fixed. All policemen who spoke freely about their fixing activities were indignant at any suggestion that they or their colleagues would accept money for their services. One lieutenant hotly replied, "If we found that one of our men was taking money for fixing, he'd be fired immediately!" None of the evidence collected either during my study or during the three-year investigations of the Massachusetts Crime Commission (which, though it concentrated on corruption at the state level, also investigated ticket fixing)[8] revealed any instances in which money was accepted to cover up a minor traffic violation. The only explanation for this is that,

7. "State's Safety Council Says 50% of Traffic Tickets Fixed," *Boston Herald*, March 23, 1965.
8. Interview with Alfred Gardner, Chairman of the Massachusetts Crime Commission, August 3, 1965.

since police chiefs are so willing to fix tickets on the basis of friendship or political influence, there is no reason to offer cash when stopped by an officer. If corruption in the sense of an exchange of money exists in the field of traffic-law enforcement—and there was no evidence that it does in Massachusetts at least —it would probably exist at the level of the chief rather than at the level of the arresting officer.

If money is not the basis of ticket fixing, why do policemen do it? For chiefs and men alike, fixing tickets is an easily effective form of patronage. One traffic officer described fixing as a kind of insurance. "If you take care of a ticket for a liquor dealer or salesman," he noted, "you can expect consideration when you go in to buy a suit or a bottle." Policemen distinguish sharply, it might be noted, between accepting a bribe and receiving consideration; to a policeman, accepting five dollars from a motorist is dishonest, but buying a suit for less than its list price is not. Ticket fixing also provides insurance of another sort. When asked why policemen were willing to fix tickets when called by policemen from another city, one officer replied, "Well, some day one of our men may want to take care of something in that city, so we'll fix this thing for them now."

For the police chief, fixing tickets also offers a means of maintaining cordial relationships with state and local politicians as well as with local citizens. One patrolman philosophically noted, "Fixing tickets is about the only thing that the chief can do for politicians." The chiefs in Cambridge and Malden were the statehouse lobbyists for, respectively, the Massachusetts Chiefs of Police Association and the Massachusetts Police Association; and both men appeared regularly at the statehouse to ask for legislative favors. All police chiefs must also appear before city councils and town boards of selectmen to ask for pay raises, new equipment, and so forth. Finally, since chiefs must deal with other chiefs, both socially at the monthly association meetings and professionally in conducting multicity crime investigations, they face pressure to honor fix requests from other chiefs and their friends. Some chiefs said that, unless they fixed tickets, they could not expect cooperation from other police forces on more serious matters (such intercity matters as escaped convicts or an auto-theft gang). This, of course, assumes that there is a basic feeling that chiefs *should* fix for their colleagues. A more plausible explanation involves a feeling of reciprocity—"I will not be able to fix one of *his* tickets for my friends if I don't take care of his friends who get *my* tickets. Besides, knowing the problems that I have with officials and politicians in my city, I don't want to cause him any extra problems with his officials and their friends."

Although ticket fixing is a practice generally accepted by chiefs and policemen, it is also a source of conflict between them. As the chief in one small town said, "You have to strike a balance between townspeople and the men on your force or you'll never get anything done." The fixing standards described earlier leave a gray area between violations which both the chief and the arresting officer agree are definitely fixable and those which are not. Under pressure from another chief or a local citizen or politician, a chief may be required to persuade the officer that the motorist was not too rude or that his speed was not too dangerous. Conflict about *who* will do the fixing may also be engendered, as it was by two aspects of the Massachusetts law in effect when my study was conducted. The chief had the choice of whether or not to give Registry ticket books to his men, and the decision whether to take a violator to court had to be made by the chief or by "an officer of a rank not lower than sergeant," not by the arresting officer.[9] Earlier I pointed out that only 28 of the 180 police chiefs gave Registry ticket books to their men; chiefs also varied in encouraging or even permitting their men to *suggest* the recommendations to be made on individual tickets. Patrolmen were angry that they were not given Registry books, and many cited instances in which recommendations they had suggested were ignored by the chief, who either downgraded requests for court summonses or upgraded suggested warnings.

While collecting information on ticketing in Massachusetts, I asked over one hundred chiefs for opinions regarding a bill then pending before the legislature which would (1) require every chief to give Registry books to his men and (2) allow the arresting officer to decide whether the motorist would receive a summons or a warning. About two thirds opposed the bill. Some of their arguments sounded farfetched: "It's hard to write a ticket in the rain." "Some of my men have poor penmanship." "Some tickets might get lost if they are carried around." "The ticket books are too heavy to carry around." Most of the chiefs, however, presented arguments founded on a basic distrust of their men. Back in 1960, "Police chiefs who opposed the no-fix system said the judgment of their officers in issuing tickets is not always good; and there are times when they have to overrule them. They feel, therefore, that this discretion should remain with department heads."[10] In 1965, the arguments were almost identical. "Some of our men have bad judgment." "If I couldn't control things in my office, those guys would be fixing tickets out on the street." "If we gave them the Registry books, they would conduct vendettas." And, finally, "If I gave them the chance, they would ticket all of my friends." The lineup of witnesses testifying on the

9. Mass. G.L. Ch. 90C §2.
10. "Legislators Support No-Fix," *Boston Herald*, March 13, 1960.

1965 no-fix bill showed the chief–patrolman split: the lobbyist for the Chiefs' Association opposed the bill; the secretary of the Police Association supported it.

A final note should be added on the subject of ticket fixing: from all available evidence, fixing is almost identical in all parts of Massachusetts and thus bears no relationship to the frequency with which police forces *write* tickets. Interviews with policemen and politicians in high-enforcement cities indicated that fixing there followed the same pattern as in the low-enforcement cities. Even more surprising is the fact that policemen on forces whose chiefs urged ticket writing felt no greater dislike of their chiefs' fixing preferences than patrolmen on the low-enforcement forces. Even the traffic men who wrote over a thousand tickets apiece in 1964 felt free to request fixes for their friends and relatives.

If traffic officers know that their chief fixes tickets and refuses to give them the Registry ticket books, why do they write tickets? The answer is that they seem to dissociate fixing from departmental pressures to write (or not write) tickets. From their limited contacts with policemen in other cities, they know that other chiefs fix tickets and refuse to give out the books. "Sure, the chief fixes," one traffic man said, "but I don't think he's as bad as some other chiefs." The answer to the question of why fixing does not bother the traffic men seems to be that they accept fixing as something that *all* chiefs do; as long as their chief does not fix a ticket in which they are *particularly* interested (when the motorist was offensive, say), they see no troublesome conflict—their day's work, to borrow a phrase used earlier, is over once the tickets have been written.

Ticket fixing, then, shows another dimension of the political context in which police chiefs must view traffic-law enforcement. While there are few general pressures against enforcement (other than budget restrictions), the chief must be prepared for calls to fix individual tickets. Although this gives him an opportunity to make friends and to build up his bargaining power when other needs arise, it can also put him in a position where he makes enemies. I quoted above the statement of a small-town police chief who had to strike a balance between townspeople and patrolmen; an order to fix a ticket falling in the "gray area" on the scale of "fixability" can antagonize members of the police force. A general willingness to fix tickets can also at times antagonize politicians. As one captain summarized his experience, "They always forget that you've fixed nine tickets for them if you have to say no to the tenth request."

7 / The Influence of Environment

My four cities were chosen because they were the cities with the highest (Waltham and Cambridge) and lowest (Lynn and Malden) rates of persons ticketed per thousand motor vehicles in the Boston area. In each chapter, certain local facts—the character of the chief and officers, departmental norms, and so forth— were offered to explain the ticketing figures. But it might be asked whether it is possible to predict the traffic policies of other police forces from information related to the environments in which they operate. Do the police, for example, react uniformly to the policies of the district courts into which they must bring traffic cases? Is the intensity of enforcement related to local traffic-accident experience? Can ticketing policies be predicted from the demographic character of the city or town?

To test these questions, I collected data from the 180 cities and towns in Massachusetts with populations greater than 5,000 and from 508 cities with over 25,000 people throughout the nation. Responses from police departments were supplemented by statistics on the court disposition of traffic cases, traffic-accident figures, automobile-insurance rates, and personal interviews.[1] In moving

1. Data on Massachusetts district courts are from Massachusetts Department of Correction, *Statistical Reports* (Boston, 1962, 1963, 1964). Unfortunately, comparable figures were not readily available for other states. Accident data for Massachusetts cities and towns are from Massachusetts Registry of Motor Vehicles, *Motor Vehicle Traffic Accidents, Injuries, and Deaths* (Boston, 1962, 1963, 1964). Accident figures for cities in other states are based on unpublished statistics collected by the National Safety Council. Automobile-insurance rates for Massachusetts cities and towns are

from the four case studies to an analysis of a state or the entire nation, we must keep in mind several weaknesses of the basic measures (tickets per thousand motor vehicles, per thousand population, and per policeman). The validity of the assumptions made in my introduction, regarding similarity of driver conduct, road patterns, the impact of commuter traffic, and traffic laws, is progressively weakened as we move into wider areas. *Some* baseline is needed, however, and so I shall continue to use these measures; the area being discussed (Massachusetts or the entire nation) will be specified at each point.

The Influence of the Courts. Earlier it was noted that police forces vary widely both in the rate at which tickets are written and in the percentage of these tickets that are referred to the courts for action. There is a major problem in trying to discover whether either of these variations can be attributed to policies of the courts with which the police must work. Although we can easily learn the results of court action (such as the percentage of defendants acquitted) and the requirements of the courts concerning the appearance of arresting officers (when the case is first called or only after the defendant pleads not guilty), it is quite possible that police forces are reacting to "the courts" but not to *these* facets of the courts; the critical court experience may well be something that can only be uncovered through intensive interviews with local lawyers, judges, or police officers. In Cambridge, for example, Chief Brennan sent few tickets to court because the court clerk's office was, he felt, too busy to issue summonses promptly. Several police chiefs in the area served by the Quincy,

contained in Massachusetts Department of Banking and Insurance, Division of Insurance, *Classification of Risks and Schedule of Premium Charges* (Boston, 1955, 1965).

Massachusetts, district court noted that one judge in that court was very slow in hearing traffic cases; officers frequently had to wait in court while the judge handled only two or three traffic cases an hour. Two police chiefs in cities outside Massachusetts attributed a decline in ticketing to a refusal on the part of local judges to convict drivers on charges of failing to yield the right of way at intersections. Several police officers in Essex County (in northeastern Massachusetts) referred to a judge who disliked either policemen or traffic cases. One officer testified in this court that he had chased a motorist doing 80 m.p.h. and had decided that the pursuit was endangering others; having obtained the license number, he stopped and radioed ahead to have the motorist arrested. "What's the matter?" the judge asked the officer, "Did you chicken out? Case dismissed." Finally, a case from the Brookline, Massachusetts, district court might be cited. For years there has been a feud between the Brookline police and the Brookline judge. At one point, the police placed parking tickets on the illegally parked cars of the judge and his son; the judge retaliated by filing (continuing without fine) all parking tickets brought into his court for the next few months.

In each of these Massachusetts court districts, the police reacted to supposed procedural deficiencies or idiosyncracies of the judge by avoiding court action in the tickets they wrote. Table 16 shows the recommendations made by the police forces in these four court districts.

Although hostility toward the courts kept these police departments from sending tickets to court, it did not necessarily cause the police to avoid *writing* tickets. Table 17 shows the number of persons ticketed per thousand motor vehicles by the municipal police forces in these four court districts.

In the absence of information of this sort—the extent of delay in issuing summonses or hearing cases, or the personal relationships between the police and particular judges—about *all* courts, we can only look to see whether ticketing policies varied uniformly in response to court policies concerning the appearance of

Table 16. Ticket Recommendations in Four Court Districts, 1964

Court	% court or arrest
Quincy	24.9
Cambridge	22.5
Salem	16.2
Brookline	4.0
All 173 cities and towns in Massachusetts for which 1964 ticket recommendations are known	58.7

Note. Brookline was the only municipality in its court district. The figures for other court districts were obtained by dividing the total number of persons brought into court by the total number of persons ticketed in 1964 by municipal police forces in cities and towns over 5,000 population in the court district. The figure for *all* cities and towns was obtained by dividing the total number of persons brought into court and arrested by the total number of persons ticketed in 173 cities and towns (7 towns over 5,000 failed to send audit sheets to the Registry).

Table 17. Persons Ticketed in Four Court Districts, 1964

Court location	Persons ticketed per 1,000 motor vehicles
Brookline	128
Cambridge	98
Salem	42
Quincy	32
180 cities and towns	56

Note. The "persons ticketed" figures were obtained by dividing the total number of persons ticketed by the total number of registered motor vehicles in all cities and towns over 5,000 population in each court district and in the state.

the arresting officer or in response to the courts' acquittal rates in traffic cases.

The Lynn and Malden police forces, as noted earlier, are required to send the arresting officer to court on the day the motorist is summoned to appear, on the "first call" of a case; arresting officers in Waltham and Cambridge, however, are only called into court if the defendant pleads not guilty. Several Massachusetts chiefs whose officers were required to appear at the first call of a case complained during interviews that a large percentage of their force was tied up while court was in session, and usually for no reason, since 85-90 percent of all motorists plead guilty. Chief Carmody of Waltham mentioned that if his court did not permit the delayed appearance of officers, he would not be able to prosecute as many violators as he does. A traffic officer in Malden, where the officer must appear at the first call, ventured the opinion that "it's court appearances that can kill a police department." Opposing legislation in 1965 which would permit a policeman to issue a court summons at the site of a traffic violation, the Massachusetts Chiefs of Police Association argued that "Court appearance of the officers issuing the citations would deplete the patrol force of many municipalities during the periods when maximum security is necessary for the safety of the community."[2]

To a policeman, the rules on court appearance have a more personal meaning. If he is on the day shift, he simply leaves his post to go to court. If he is on the afternoon or night shift, however, he must come to court during his off-hours; *if* he testifies (if the motorist contests the charges), he will receive a witness fee (usually $3). The possibility of receiving $3 may seem to the

2. Letter from the Traffic and Safety Committee of the Massachusetts Chiefs of Police Association to members of the Massachusetts Legislature, February 1965.

officer to be inadequate compensation for the sleep and leisure time lost while in court. But if he knows that he will only have to appear in court on the 10-15 percent of his tickets that will be contested, he may feel freer to write tickets. The chief of one small thirteen-man force felt that its ticketing had increased by 25 percent during 1964 simply because the judge of their court changed his mind and decided to allow deferred appearances; the night-shift officers who had previously refused to write tickets were now willing to do so.[3]

If the question of court appearance seems so important to both chiefs and policemen, we should ask how it affected their ticketing activities. The percentage of tickets marked for court action (including persons arrested) in the 62 not-guilty cities and towns in Massachusetts was 61.3 per cent; in 111 first-call municipalities in the state, the figure was 54.8 percent—7 percent lower than in the not-guilty cities and towns.[4] Table 18 shows that in all sizes of municipalities in Massachusetts, the first-call–not-guilty distinction also had a significant impact on the number of persons ticketed by police departments. When we look at cities throughout the United States, we find, as was noted in the introduction,

3. The impact of court-appearance rules on the arresting practices of various types of enforcement officers is noted in American Bar Foundation, *The Administration of Criminal Justice in the United States: Pilot Project Report,* II (Chicago: American Bar Foundation, 1957), 288—Detroit traffic police; James Q. Wilson, "The Police and the Delinquent in Two Cities," in *City Politics and Public Policy* (New York: Wiley, 1968)— juvenile officers in two cities; and Steven V. Roberts, "Wasted Time Cut in Housing Court," *New York Times,* June 19, 1966—New York building inspectors.

4. In each category, the total number of persons summoned into court (or arrested) was divided by the total number of persons ticketed. Seven first-call police forces failed to send ticket-book audit sheets to the Registry of Motor Vehicles; so the distribution of ticket recommendations could not be determined.

Table 18. Persons Ticketed per 1,000 Motor Vehicles in Not-Guilty and First-Call Municipalities in Massachusetts

Size of city or Town	Persons ticketed per 1,000 motor vehicles		
	Not guilty	First call	Difference
5,000– 9,999 (59)	54	44	10
10,000–19,999 (66)	54	39	15
20,000–49,999 (34)	48	31	17
50,000 and over (21)	113	41	72
All cities and towns (180)	84	38	46
	(n = 62)	(n = 118)	

Note. In each size and category, the figure was calculated by dividing the total number of persons ticketed by the total number of registered motor vehicles.

much higher rates of ticketing than in Massachusetts alone, but the distinction regarding court appearance still remains. The mean of 124 first-call cities was 164 tickets per thousand motor vehicles; the mean of 349 not-guilty cities was 191 tickets per thousand vehicles.[5]

Apart from the court-appearance variable, no strong relationship could be found between police ticketing and court policies. It might have been expected, for example, that a police force

5. These figures represent the *mean* of the ticketing *rates* for all cities in the group rather than the figures for all tickets divided by all motor vehicles in these cities. Using the other measures of the intensity of ticketing, the comparable figures are:

	Tickets per policeman	*Tickets per 1,000 population*
All cities	$\bar{X} = 69$, $s = 55$ (N = 508)	$\bar{X} = 105$, $s = 87$ (N = 508)
First-call cities	$\bar{X} = 57$, $s = 55$ (N = 126)	$\bar{X} = 87$, $s = 82$ (N = 126)
Not-guilty cities	$\bar{X} = 74$, $s = 55$ (N = 353)	$\bar{X} = 110$, $s = 89$ (N = 353)

would write fewer tickets or would send fewer motorists to court
if its district court acquitted a high percentage of defendants in
traffic cases; in fact, the Pearsonian correlation coefficients were
less than .20 when the percentage of traffic case acquittals in
Massachusetts courts was compared with either the number of
persons ticketed per thousand motor vehicles or with the percentage of tickets marked for court action. (The range of acquittal rates was in fact quite small; 71 of the 73 district courts
convicted more than 90 percent of the defendants in traffic cases;
the other two courts convicted between 80 percent and 90 percent.) The coefficients were similarly low when ticketing and
ticket recommendations were compared with acquittals in those
cases in which the defendants pleaded not guilty. Since no state-
wide agency collects information on the *size* of fines imposed in
traffic cases, it was impossible to compare police-ticketing activities with court-imposed penalties.

The Influence of Traffic Accidents. Police chiefs frequently
state that they assign men to look for traffic violations in response
to local accident experience. Chief Carmody of Waltham, for
example, noted that he had assigned extra men to enforcement
work following a spectacular fatal accident early in 1965. Several
chiefs who said that their 1964 ticketing was much higher than
that of previous years cited increased accidents as the basis for
decisions to encourage their men to write more tickets. Waltham
officers also noted that insurance rates had improved in recent
years and that citizens were giving them the credit for it.

To a large extent, evaluating the relation between accidents
and ticketing policies presents the same problem involved in
handling court data. Just as an egregious error by a judge (as in
the case of the judge who dismissed charges brought by the

policeman who "chickened out") can turn a police force against a judge, even though his usual actions (*rates* of acquittal or severity of fines) are favorable to them, so may one spectacular accident have a greater impact upon a police department than a comparatively high *rate* of personal-injury or property-damage accidents. Since it is impossible to know for each city in the nation whether specific accidents in recent years have been more distressing (such as the death of a child) or have received more publicity, we can only use general measures of accidents. This raises the question of *which* measure of accidents should be used; in 1963, for example, Massachusetts was the third *safest* state in the nation (tied with New Jersey behind Connecticut and Rhode Island) in terms of highway fatalities per 100 million vehicle miles traveled,[6] but it had the *worst* record in the nation in terms of "the number of (insurance) claims paid for bodily injury and property damage resulting from automobile accidents."[7] To compensate for this variation in results, the Massachusetts figures on persons ticketed per thousand motor vehicles were compared with data from the Registry of Motor Vehicles on fatalities, personal injuries, and property-damage accidents in excess of $200, and with insurance rates (based on claims made by residents of the municipality rather than on accidents occurring in the municipality). Ticketing figures from cities outside Massachusetts were compared with National Safety Council figures on fatal and personal-injury accidents.

By *none* of these measures was local accident experience significantly correlated with police-ticketing figures. The Pearsonian

6. National Safety Council, *Accident Facts* (Chicago: National Safety Council, 1964).

7. Based on a study prepared by the Insurance Institute for Highway Safety, quoted in Wendell Coltin, "State Leading in Accident Claims," *Boston Herald*, June 20, 1965.

r correlation coefficient[8] in the case of the average number of persons killed in Massachusetts cities in the years 1961 through 1963 was .12. The correlation with the average number of accidents of all types (fatal, personal injury, and property damage) in Massachusetts in this period was .11. (Correlations were similarly low when the number of fatalities or accidents was divided by the number of motor vehicles registered in the city or town.) The correlation with automobile insurance rates in Massachusetts cities was .09.

The unreliability of accident data as predictors of ticketing policies is illustrated by Table 19, which presents accident figures from the four cities analyzed in Part One. Although the data on *fatal* accidents parallel increases in ticketing rates, on the basis of many of the other accident figures, highest-ticketing Waltham was closest to lowest-ticketing Lynn; so it is difficult to argue either that accidents produced high (or low) ticketing or that ticketing produced a high (or low) accident rate.

The Influence of Police-Department Variables. In the last chapter we shall look at the significance of police policies regarding the organization of traffic-law enforcement within the department, the degree of tolerance with which traffic laws should be enforced (for instance, whether tickets should be written when the motorist is exceeding the speed limit by one, ten, or twenty miles per hour), the actions that are encouraged (production of a "quota" of tickets as against "courtesy to motorists," say), and so forth. Before leaving the statistical data, however, we might look

8. The Pearsonian *r* correlation coefficient measures the degree of dispersion of points around a regression line. It varies from 0 to 1; coefficient approaching 1.0 indicate a strong relationship between two variables, while coefficients approaching 0.0 indicate a weak relationship. Negative relationships between two variables are indicated by negative coefficients (e.g., —.40).

to see if ticketing policies are related to certain aspects of the formal organization of these police departments.

Several officials of the Massachusetts Registry of Motor Vehicles and the Massachusetts Safety Council expressed the opinion that police officers who were not protected by the civil-service system would be less likely to write traffic tickets than

Table 19. Accident Statistics from Four Cities

Statistics	Lynn	Malden	Cambridge	Waltham
1960 population	94,478	57,676	107,716	55,413
Average traffic fatalities, 1961–1964	2.3	4.0	7.3	5.7
Fatalities per 1,000 motor vehicles	.06	.16	.19	.18
Average 1961–63 accidents of all types	1,290	803	2,088	909
Average accidents per 1,000 motor vehicles	30.6	32.5	54.7	29.4
1965 insurance rate	$66	$77	$77	$50
1955–1965 increase in insurance rate	$22	$26	$26	$13
Persons ticketed in 1964 per 1,000 motor vehicles	11.9	16.8	143.0	158.3

those who were. Policemen who lack the protection of civil-service tenure, they argued, fear that if they antagonize local citizens by writing tickets, they will quickly be out of a job. When Massachusetts cities and towns were divided according to the civil-service status of their police forces, however, it appeared that 39 percent (8) of the non-civil-service forces ticketed less than 30 persons per thousand motor vehicles; 33 percent (27) of the civil-service forces ticketed this few. Nine percent (2) of the non-civil-service forces ticketed more than 100 persons per thousand motor vehicles; 13 percent (18) of the forces protected by civil service wrote this many tickets. It is thus hard to say that civil-service status alone made much difference in the ticketing attitudes of policemen.

It will be recalled that the chief in Lynn expressed the opinion that he didn't have enough men to assign one to traffic-enforcement work on a full-time basis. We also noted that the chief did have enough men to assign one to traffic work when irate citizens demanded action at particular locations. Although we have no way of measuring all of the duties that were given to police forces in 1964, we might get a rough estimate of police-department workloads by looking at the number of police officers per thousand population and the recent crime rate in the city. In Massachusetts cities and towns, the correlation coefficient was .14 when ticketing figures were compared with the number of police officers per thousand population; the figure for 508 American cities was .16.[9] When ticketing figures were compared with the number of crimes known to the police in 1963 per thousand population, the coefficient for Massachusetts cities was .12; for 508 American cities, the figure was .34—a positive correlation suggesting that ticketing is *higher* in cities with a greater crime problem. So a heavy workload, at least as measured by crimes or police per capita, cannot be used to explain police reluctance to allocate resources to traffic enforcement. But it will be noted

9. Data on the size of police forces was obtained through letters sent to police chiefs. Since police departments vary in recruitment and job-classification practices, some may have included clerical or maintenance personnel in their reports while others listed only uniformed officers. Since no alternate sources of information are available, these self-reported figures are used, even though they may not be exactly comparable.

shortly that a high crime rate is associated with conditions under which the police will be likely to take a strict or formalistic view of violations (writing tickets) rather than a lenient or informal view (ignoring violators or giving them warnings).

One final police-department variable might be mentioned at this point, even though available data are insufficient to discuss it adequately. This concerns the distribution of receipts from traffic fines. In some American cities, all or a portion of these fines are given to the police department; in others, the city or county treasuries are enriched. Unfortunately, it was impossible to collect information on this variable for all of the cities studied, and thus it is impossible either to confirm or to reject the popular opinion that police departments which "profit" directly from ticketing will be more zealous than those which do not benefit from fines. It should be remembered, however, that there was a wide variety of ticketing policies within Massachusetts, where *none* of the police departments collected the fines (fines from violations of state laws went to the counties; fines from violations of local ordinances went to the cities and towns in which the violations occurred).

Demographic Characteristics and Ticketing Policies. These analyses of court and accident data suggest that the police do not vary their enforcement policies in response to local accident or court-acquittal rates, although specific incidents—a hostile judge or a spectacular accident—may lead to policy changes. To conclude this discussion of the influence of environment upon traffic policies, it might be asked whether these policies are correlated in any way with characteristics of the residents of the communities in which the police operate. Recent studies have, for example, found moderate correlations between demographic characteristics and local governmental structure, urban renewal, fluoridation, and expenditure policies.[10]

In my introduction the four cities were described in terms of census variables and the Williams and Adrian typology of local government. It will be recalled, from Table 6, that Waltham was somewhat more prosperous than Malden and Lynn, and that Cambridge contained both a sizable professional group and a large working-class population. We also noted, in Table 7, that the four cities differed in certain political characteristics, with the low-tax, low-expenditure caretaker philosophy predominating in Lynn and Malden, the economic-growth role favored in Waltham, and an arbiter group mediating between economic-growth and caretaker factions in Cambridge.

Although one cannot identify dominant political patterns for each city without extensive field research, and although the crudeness of census data as indicators of the nature of a community adds to the weaknesses inherent in my measures of police ticketing policies, we might look briefly at correlation and re-

10. See the articles cited by Lewis A. Froman, "An Analysis of Public Policies in Cities," *Journal of Politics,* XXIX (February 1967), 94–108; Amos Hawley, "Community Power and Urban Renewal Success," *American Journal of Sociology,* LXVIII (January 1963), 422–431, and see the critical response to Hawley by Bruce C. Straits, "Community Adoption and Implementation of Urban Renewal," *American Journal of Sociology,* LXXI (July 1965), 77–82; Maurice Pinard, "Structural Attachment and Political Support in Urban Politics: The Case of Fluoridation Referendums," *American Journal of Sociology,* LXVIII (March 1963), 513–526; Oliver P. Williams, Harold Herman, Charles S. Liebman, and Thomas R. Dye, *Suburban Differences and Metropolitan Policies: A Philadelphia Story* (Philadelphia: University of Pennsylvania Press, 1965); Robert C. Wood, *1400 Governments* (Cambridge: Harvard University Press, 1961); and Louis H. Massotti and Don R. Bowen, "Communities and Budgets: The Sociology of Municipal Expenditures," *Urban Affairs Quarterly,* I (December 1965), 39–58.

gression figures from both Massachusetts cities and my sample of 508 United States police forces. For the 180 Massachusetts cities and towns with a 1960 population greater than 5,000, the Pearsonian r correlation coefficient never rose above (plus or minus) .12 when the number of persons ticketed per thousand motor vehicles was compared with income (median family income or percent of families with income below $3,000 or above $10,000), education (median school years completed, percent with less than five years of schooling, or percent of high-school graduates), employment (percent unemployed, percent in professional occupations or percent in craftsmen occupations), housing (median rent, median value of single-unit houses, percent of housing units owner-occupied, age of housing units), and ethnic data (percent foreign-born or with foreign or mixed parentage) from the 1960 Census. The correlation with the percent of non-whites was .29.

Looking at 508 American cities larger than 25,000, on *none* of the measures of ticketing (tickets per thousand motor vehicles, tickets per policeman, and tickets per thousand population) were there correlations greater than plus or minus .20 with measures of income or education. The same was true for measures of ethnicity and housing. Whereas these demographic variables, both from Massachusetts cities and from the sample of American cities, offer little explanation for police ticketing policies, a number of moderately strong correlations appear when ticketing rates are compared with several indicators of the stability of the 508 cities' populations, territorial mobility, age of the population, change in the city's size, and the incidence of serious crimes.

The shape of the relationship between population stability and ticketing policies is indicated by the accompanying figure, plotting tickets per thousand motor vehicles against the percent of the city's population residing in the same house in 1960 as in

Table 20. Product-Moment Correlations Between Ticketing and Population Stability

Indicators	Tickets per 1,000 vehicles	Tickets per policeman	Tickets per 1,000 population
Stability			
% native of state	r = −.39	r = −.44	r = −.47
% same house, 1955–1960	−.36	−.45	−.43
% over age 65	−.23	−.31	−.20
Instability			
% new house since 1958	.35	.44	.40
% different county, 1955–1960	.25	.38	.34
% population change, 1955–1960	.15	.24	.19
1963 FBI crimes per 1,000 population	.34	.26	.42

Sources. 1963 FBI Crimes per 1,000 population were obtained from the 1963 *Uniform Crime Reports* (Washington: Government Printing Office, 1964). All other figures come from the 1960 Census of Populations.

1955. Using multiple regression analysis, five variables (percent in the same house, total population, crimes per capita, percent nonwhite, and percent over sixty-five) produced a multiple r of .52 with tickets per thousand motor vehicles, explaining 27 percent of the total variance.[11] To guard against the possibility that

11. The relative contributions of these variables to the total r are indicated in the following tabulation:

Variable	Multiple r	Increase in r
% in same house 1955–1960	.3610	.3610
Total 1960 population	.4414	.0804
Crimes per capita	.4853	.0439
% Non-white	.5043	.0190
% over 65	.5161	.0118

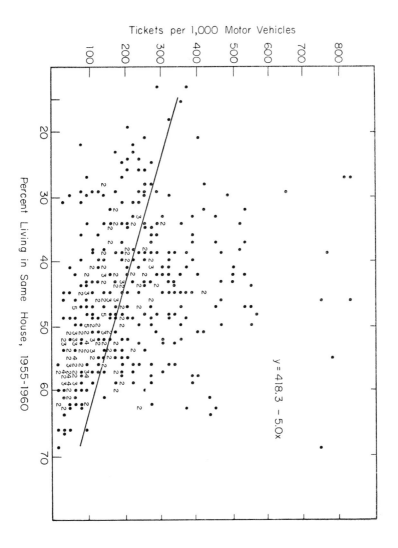

some other demographic variable associated with stability was influencing these correlations, partial correlations were also obtained. The partial correlation between tickets per policeman and percent living in the same house in 1960 as in 1955 (simple correlation, —.45) was —.38 when controlled for median school years, —.46 when controlled for median family income, and —.46 when controlled for percent in white-collar occupations. Stability, therefore, had an independent role in producing correlations with ticketing.

What conclusions can we draw from these data? One explanation for the correlation between ticketing rates and indicators of stability might be that residents in rapidly changing cities *expect* their police forces to act differently (more strictly) than residents in more stable communities. A parallel relationship between stability and attitudes toward local government has been hypothesized by Robert Alford and Harry Scoble. Looking at the form of government of all American cities with over 25,000 people, they found that population mobility (here, the percent living in a different county in 1960 than in 1955) was the best predictor of whether a city would have a council-manager rather than a mayor-council form of government.[12] Assuming that the mayor-council form "encourages or allows interest-group representation" and that the council-manager form "encourages efficient implementation of specified goals," Alford and Scoble hypothesize that population growth and mobility are "intervening variables, serving to loosen the social and political ties of persons to their community and rendering ineffective those characteristics of the

12. Robert R. Alford and Harry M. Scoble, "Political and Socioeconomic Characteristics of American Cities," *1965 Municipal Yearbook* (Chicago: International City Managers' Association, 1965), pp. 82–97. Mobility remained the best predictor of the form of local government even after partialling for region, occupation, population change, and city size.

population which would otherwise bring forth political demands."[13] In highly mobile cities, therefore, where political interests have not yet become organized, the goal of efficiency will predominate and be reflected in the city-manager form of government. The parallel hypothesis might be offered that, in the absence of political demands to enforce laws with reference to persons, the police will be expected to enforce criminal laws strictly (with reference to rules); further, just as the stabilization of a population produces demands that can be satisfied more readily through a mayor-council form of government, so will stabilization produce demands for the "political" enforcement of criminal laws. Strict law enforcement might thus be expected in the newer, more mobile communities where countervailing political pressures have not yet developed.

It might be reassuring to democratic theorists to conclude that police policies are formed on the basis of such community attitudes, but I doubt that this explanation of the correlation and regression figures is accurate. The proposition that police enforcement policies would parallel variations in the community because of varying community expectations of the police demands as-

13. *Ibid.*, p. 96. Interestingly, ticketing also varies with the form of government in the 508 cities, as is suggested in the following figures, condensed somewhat from a larger table on which the subsequent statistics are based.

Form of government		Tickets per 1,000 motor vehicles				
	0–99	100–199	200–299	300–399	400+	Total
Mayor-council	89	59	17	14	15	194
Commission	23	15	7	3	—	48
Council-manager	47	74	73	29	25	248
	159	148	97	46	40	490

$X^2 = 107.59$; Pearson's contingency coefficient $C = .42$

sumptions that people in the community care whether traffic laws are enforced strictly or leniently, that these popular attitudes vary according to social class or some other demographic grouping, and that the police know of and carry out these community-based policies.

Even if it is accurate to say that people in a community care what traffic policies their police follow, there are several reasons why we should *not* expect to find correlations between attitudes toward ticketing and demographic characteristics. First, in a nation so generally tied to the automobile, all citizens may have similar attitudes toward traffic-law enforcement—attitudes simultaneously desiring traffic safety and the avoidance of tickets. Early declarations that the traffic violation was primarily a "white collar" crime have been seriously questioned.[14] And though different traffic laws may hit different social classes—lower-class drivers are more likely to violate safety equipment and insurance regulations while upper-class drivers are more frequently arrested for driving under the influence[15]—members of all classes may be equally (and equally ambiguously) interested in whether the local police will give them a ticket or save them from accidents.

More important than the probable similarity of attitudes toward traffic-law enforcement in all cities is the fact that, as stressed in Chapter Six, local residents know little about their police force's traffic policies. Although residents may observe

14. H. Laurence Ross, "Traffic Law Violation—A Folk Crime," *Social Problems*, VIII (Winter 1960–61), 231–241, reports that the proportion of white-collar workers arrested for traffic violations is higher than that involved in other types of crime, but also that they are represented among those arrested for this type of crime roughly in proportion to their numbers in the community (here, Evanston, Illinois).

15. T. C. Willett, *Criminal on the Road: A Study of Motoring Offenses and Those Who Commit Them* (London: Tavistock, 1964), pp. 194–199.

individual officers writing tickets (or ignoring violations), they are unlikely to know (and the police force probably hopes they will not discover) what proportion of the force is assigned to traffic, what areas of the city are being watched, or what tolerance levels (miles per hour above the speed limit before a ticket will be written) are being enforced.[16]

If it is thus unlikely that the statistical relationship between demographic stability and ticketing policies stems from variations in community attitudes toward the police, it is more reasonable to conclude that stability influences police attitudes toward the public. The police in a stable community, particularly in a smaller city or town, are likely to take a more lenient, nonticketing attitude toward violators than police in more mobile or unstable cities. Several factors underlie this relationship. The first, particularly significant in smaller communities, concerns political pressures: a patrolman or chief may fear that citizen resentment against a ticket or a "crackdown" will lead to budgetary or other reprisals from local officials. Where the community is larger, or where population mobility reduces the political power of individual citizens, the impact of this constraint will diminish.

A more pervasive aspect of the relationship between demographic stability and police attitudes concerns familiarity with the "clientele" population. The chief of one thirteen-man department in Massachusetts argued that since he knew all six thousand of the people in his community, he did not have to write traffic tickets—he could lecture violators and threaten to have

16. This is not to suggest that local residents know particularly less about the police than about other local bureaucracies; knowledge about *all* local agencies is low. See Morris Janowitz, Deil Wright, and William Delaney, *Public Administration and the Public—Perspectives toward Government in a Metropolitan Community*, Michigan Governmental Study No. 36 (Ann Arbor: University of Michigan Institute of Public Administration, 1958).

their drivers' licenses suspended if they were apprehended again. A high-ranking administrator of a large midwestern police department surmised that population mobility and community size could affect police attitudes (such as the decision whether to write a ticket or to deliver a verbal warning) both specifically— the likelihood that the officer would know *this* motorist would diminish as the size and mobility of the population increased— and generally—the policeman in the small, settled community would have a greater sense of identification with local residents than would the large-city officer.

These figures thus suggest that, as the level of demographic stability decreases, police officers observing violations will tend to rely more upon formal actions (arrests or tickets). This conclusion would appear to be supported by the work of Michael Banton who, after studying two Scottish and three American police forces, concluded that there was a direct relationship between the level of social integration (the level of consensus or agreement on fundamental values) and the utility of informal sanctions against lawbreakers. Police in more integrated cities, he argues, feel that informal controls will produce desired changes in conduct and thus are less likely to impose formal sanctions; where the agreement on fundamental values is lower, the police may well feel that only formal sanctions will be effective.[17] An example of this response can be found in the tendency, noted earlier, for police to issue tickets to abusive motorists; such conduct, the police say, indicates disrespect for the law and thus a probability that only formal measures will be effective. Since there is a fairly strong ($-.47$) negative correlation between the stability of population (here, the percent born in the same state)

17. Michael Banton, *The Policeman in the Community* (London: Tavistock, 1964), pp. 3, 136–137.

and FBI crimes per thousand population, it would not be totally unreasonable to conclude that policemen expect better results from informal sanctions in older, more settled communities than in communities with rapidly changing populations.[18]

18. The correlation between population mobility and crime rates might suggest that the police in more mobile communities might be working with a greater rate of traffic violations per thousand vehicles, per thousand population, per policeman, and thus that the seeming differences noted earlier do not really exist—that the police forces are in fact responding similarly to varying rates of violation of traffic laws. When the relationship between ticketing (tickets per policeman) and mobility (percent native of the same state)—simple $r = -.44$—is controlled for crimes per thousand population, however, the correlation remains high ($-.36$).

8 / Police Discretion and Effective Rates of Law Enforcement

> The formal, legal system seems to assume that police will arrest all who violate the criminal law . . . In fact the process is much more complicated than it is in theory. Police, in the process of allocating limited enforcement resources, exercise a very great influence upon the decision as to what conduct is to be subjected to the criminal process.[1]

The legal system assumes a simple and clear-cut role for the police: apprehend any person who violates any law. As traffic laws are in fact administered, however, a number of policies can be seen which run contrary to our goal of the equal treatment of individuals. It is easy, of course, to evaluate ticket fixing: we feel that it is unjust to base police practices on the political or social status of violators. We also feel that it is unjust (or at least unrelated to the ends of justice) when enforcement decisions are based upon personal feuds, as between a police chief and a local judge.

A third form of the unjust administration of traffic laws by the police concerns the harassment of particular groups of motorists. Unlike some other areas of law enforcement, this does *not* involve discrimination against minority groups or the poor, except insofar

1. Frank J. Remington and Victor G. Rosenblum, "The Criminal Law and the Legislative Process," *University of Illinois Law Forum* (Winter 1960), p. 496.

as traffic laws require expensive equipment or insurance coverage.[2] The two groups that are systematically discriminated against regarding traffic—teenagers and motorists who respond abusively when stopped by an officer—exhibit conduct, unrelated to traffic, which is regarded as offensive by the police. Even when no particular violation can be charged against a teenager, Massachusetts policemen frequently write traffic tickets and ask the Registry of Motor Vehicles (not the courts) to suspend licenses. Registry files contain many tickets citing no violation but simply stating, "improper operator," "drag racing," "obscene language," "noisy," or "driving to a riot."[3] Persons who have been abusive to officers, as we have noted, are more likely than others to receive a ticket and are also ineligible to fix tickets.[4]

Two other sources of variations in the enforcement of traffic laws present greater problems of evaluation. These are variations in the application of police discretion (decisions by individual

2. H. Lawrence Ross, in "Traffic Law Violation: A Folk Crime," *Social Problems*, VIII (Winter 1960–1961), 231–241, notes that the class distribution of a sample of traffic violators paralleled the class distribution of the community studied (Evanston, Illinois).

3. For an example of a *refusal* by a police force to harass teenage drivers, see "Five-Man Police Force Quits over Orders To Harass Youths," *New York Times*, March 12, 1965.

4. The impact of abusive conduct in causing the policeman to act more severely and with more personal involvement is noted by William A. Westley, "The Police: A Sociological Study of Law, Custom, and Morality" (unpublished Ph.D. dissertation, University of Chicago, 1951); Westley, "Violence and the Police," *American Journal of Sociology*, CIX (July 1953), 34–41; Westley, "Secrecy and the Police," *Social Forces*, XXXIV (March 1956), 254–257; Wayne R. LaFave, *Arrest: The Decision To Take a Suspect into Custody* (Boston: Little, Brown, 1965) p. 146; and Joseph Goldstein, "Police Discretion Not To Invoke the Criminal Process: Low-Visibility Decisions in the Administration of Justice," *Yale Law Journal*, LXIX (March 1960), 543–594. See also Murray Edelman, *The Symbolic Uses of Politics* (Urbana: University of Illinois Press, 1964), pp. 46–47.

policemen whether or not to invoke the criminal process against observed violators) and variations in department traffic policies (organizational decisions concerning the importance of traffic work, the proportion of departmental resources to be allocated to it, and the guidelines issued to patrolmen concerning tolerance levels). Though not the primary focus of this study, variations among individual patrolmen were quite evident in the cities studied: some men disliked traffic work, others enjoyed it for various reasons, and the rest were neutral. Lynn's Officer O'Donnell wrote tickets despite a general departmental hostility toward traffic work; some men in Cambridge and Waltham only wrote tickets when harrassed by Chief Brennan or Captain Thomas. Other policemen develop a stricter attitude toward traffic violations following specialized training courses, although none of the patrolmen in the four Massachusetts cities had attended special seminars on traffic enforcement, such as those sponsored by the state police or the Traffic Institute of Northwestern University.

Going beyond special training or personal attitudes toward traffic safety is the matter of specialization. We noted in the case studies that men who were told that their *only* function was to be traffic enforcement usually wrote more tickets than general-duty patrolmen, both absolutely and per hour devoted to traffic; the generalists were less likely to write tickets even during the time they were not involved in other duties. The director of the Traffic Institute of Northwestern University has argued that "the best organizational facility for [traffic control] is highly trained, specialized forces. Except in a few instances, the general patrol forces are incapable of the function because of lack of training, administrative skill, and competent, interested supervision."[5] The

5. Franklin Kreml, "The Specialized Traffic Division," *Annals*, CCXCI (January 1954), 71.

case studies suggest that this statement is correct, but for the wrong reasons. Although special education and training are necessary for traffic engineering and accident investigation, a patrolman can be told in an hour or so how to use a stop watch to gauge speed over a measured distance, and he will know with no training when a car has come to a full stop at a stop sign. The significance of the specialization of the traffic-enforcement function is rather that, when writing tickets is the only duty of a policeman, the number of tickets written becomes the sole measure of his "work product"; a general-duty patrolman can list items other than tickets (number of doors checked, pedestrians assisted, and such) to show that he has kept busy. Even without any active coercion from superiors and even without any personal sense of mission or ideological attachment to traffic work, specialized traffic officers will write more tickets than nonspecialists just to prove that they are on the job.[6]

Policies and Equality in Enforcement. When variations among police officers, whether based on personal interests, special train-

6. Cf. Herman Goldstein, "Police Discretion: The Ideal versus the Real," *Public Administration Review*, XXIII (September 1963), 143: "Discretion may be exercised on the basis of a police officer's particular assignment. Many police agencies have officers assigned to specific types of investigations, such as those relating to homicide, burglaries, or narcotics. Officers so assigned understandably consider their respective specialized function as being of greatest importance to the department. The generalization can be made that police officers frequently refrain from invoking the criminal process for conduct which is considered of less seriousness than that which they are primarily responsible for investigating. A group of officers, intent on solving a homicide, for example, will complain bitterly of the lack of prostitutes on the streets from whom they may obtain information. Narcotic detectives will likewise make frequent use of gamblers and may even tolerate petty larcenies and minor drug violations on the part of their informants. Whatever the merits of the practice, the goal is an acceptable one: that of solving the more serious crime."

ing, or specific assignments, produce inequalities such that some violators will be prosecuted while others are warned or ignored simply because they were seen by different officers, serious questions arise about the rule of law and equality in the administration of justice—persons equally guilty are not being prosecuted equally by the police. We have still to consider, however, those intercity variations in effective rates of traffic-law enforcement which stem from deliberate police policies—decisions concerning the allocation of departmental resources to traffic rather than some other department function, an emphasis on courtesy rather than strictness, and policies regarding tolerance levels. In Table 1 we noted the total variation among police forces throughout the United States; Table 21 shows the extent to which ticketing rates vary among cities in the same state, describing the central tendency and extent of dispersion among police forces in the twenty-seven states from which five or more police forces in cities larger than 25,000 reported 1964 ticket figures.

Although variations among individual police officers, leading to the varying use of discretionary powers, probably produce some differences among cities in the effective level of ticketing, it is unlikely that discretion-induced variations are a major component of the gross variations within states shown in Table 21. That departmental policies outweigh individual preferences in producing each city's effective level of enforcement can be seen in cities that deliberately change their traffic policies. Cambridge's Chief Brennan and Waltham's Captain Thomas, for example, were able to increase ticketing rates without significant personnel changes. In Chicago, following a series of scandals, the number of tickets written by the police department fell from 570,000 in 1959 to 355,000 in 1960. After traffic-conscious O. W. Wilson was named superintendent in 1960, traffic enforcement was required of both traffic and district police, and the totals rose to 681,000 in 1962.[7] Finally, the chief of a twenty-eight-man po-

Table 21. Intrastate Variations in Ticketing Rates

State	Number of cities over 25,000 reporting	Tickets per 1,000 motor vehicles			
		Range	Median	Mean	Standard deviation
Connecticut	10	13–142	53	59	35
Massachusetts	48	4–211	36	47	42
Tennessee	6	80–387	92	169	43
Colorado	6	139–265	244	230	44
Minnesota	9	78–213	153	149	49
Rhode Island	5	28–266	185	161	49
Iowa	11	39–213	113	113	52
Indiana	14	28–263	75	91	55
North Carolina	10	81–248	157	158	55
New Jersey	24	22–218	125	108	56
Kansas	5	129–300	163	181	62
Virginia	10	80–278	191	196	66
New York	26	14–402	55	98	81
Pennsylvania	18	8–378	63	83	85
Ohio	25	14–422	163	175	109
Alabama	6	63–354	167	194	113
Washington	7	107–467	187	214	113
Wisconsin	19	52–338	99	126	121
Florida	11	40–482	287	279	126
California	64	80–815	259	290	128
Missouri	11	40–495	153	192	131
Oklahoma	7	64–525	165	213	143
Illinois	28	33–745	139	183	149
Texas	26	86–769	274	306	152
Michigan	28	91–773	286	320	153
Louisiana	7	38–542	166	199	154
Georgia	7	80–822	155	269	241

7. See "Chicago Record Again Proves 'Three E' Powers," *Chicago Traffic Safety Review* (January–February 1963).

lice department in a midwestern suburb gave this explanation of why his men wrote 881 tickets in 1963 and 3,605 in 1964:

> Since we are a small department . . . we felt that we could not afford to become specialists, but rather we had to become generalists. Hence we set about the task of making *all* officers traffic enforcement conscious . . . Officers are never required to fill a quota where traffic tickets are concerned, but are simply ordered to enforce existing laws vigorously.
>
> The Inspector's Office maintains a breakdown of daily records on all police personnel relative to their activities. These records, of course, almost immediately put the finger on the "goldbrick," or one who is not doing his job to full capacity. In this event, the officer in question is ordered into the Inspector's Office where comparative records are made available to him and efforts are made to determine reasons for the officer's lack of initiative. If the conference does not procure the desired results, further and more severe disciplinary action usually follows.[8]

These examples also show that departmental policies can have a greater impact on the perspective of individual officers than such formal factors as a traffic rather than general-duty assignment. As has been succinctly noted by Chester Barnard, "In considerable measure, specialization is a reflection of desired ends."[9] The Waltham and Cambridge chiefs wanted tickets written and assigned men to do only that. The Malden chief, though he wanted to assign men to "traffic," did not particularly want tickets

8. Letter to the author from a Missouri police chief, February 23, 1966 (emphasis in original).

9. Chester Barnard, *The Functions of the Executive* (Cambridge: Harvard University Press, 1938), p. 135.

written; Malden traffic men investigate accidents and guard school crossings in addition to looking for violations. On the other hand, in Chicago, following O. W. Wilson's renewal of emphasis on traffic, the general-duty officers began to write more tickets (in absolute numbers, not per man) than the specialists in the division.

As compared with the four forms of unequal enforcement of traffic laws previously discussed—ticket fixing, personal feuds, harassment of specific groups of motorists, and variations in attitude among individual officers—variations in department policies are probably the source of the greatest intercity variations in effective enforcement rates. What factors enter into the decisions behind these policies? To a great extent, the policies are formed by the conscious or unconscious judgments of the police chief and other superior officers regarding the totality of the responsibilities given to them by the city or state. In determining how much of his resources to allocate to traffic enforcement, the chief must decide how many men should be assigned to this work, what part of overtime funds can be used for enforcement, whether men can be spared to testify in court if officers must appear, and so forth. Chiefs must decide whether to employ their limited capacity for the "harassment" of their men in order to secure a greater production of traffic tickets or to secure some other goal. The small-town chief quoted in Chapter Six, for example, noted that in fixing tickets he was trading one resource (the confidence of his men) to gain another (citizen support).

In some cities, police chiefs choose to allocate all of their resources for the prevention and solution of more serious crimes and thus ignore traffic work. When asked to compare their ticketing record over recent years, several police chiefs, particularly in smaller departments, attributed a decline in ticketing between

1963 and 1964 to an increase in other duties. "We had to pull men off traffic and put them on night shift to cut the crime rate." "The department had more criminal work, and so took officers off patrol for investigation." "We had to spend more man-hours on other crimes." (Unfortunately, it was impossible to tell whether these "increases" in crime were objectively correct or instead reflected a changing perception by the chief of his various responsibilities. The number of tickets per thousand motor vehicles in 180 Massachusetts cities and towns showed a correlation coefficient of only —.08 when compared with the 1953–1963 increase in crimes known to the police.)

Differing resource allocations, in addition to affecting the total effort directed toward apprehending traffic violators, can also affect the action taken against them. We have frequently noted that, when the district courts require an officer to appear on the first call of a traffic case, the police will be less likely to write tickets or to bring ticketed violators into court. In addition, where the courts are slow or busy, police chiefs may choose to use the Registry of Motor Vehicles (or its counterpart in other states) for punitive action.[10]

My case studies indicate that these variations in traffic-enforcement policies can be explained only to a limited extent by such environmental variables as political pressures, demographic characteristics, or court conviction and accident rates. Although a high

10. See also Goldstein, pp. 140–148; Lon L. Fuller, *The Morality of Law* (New Haven: Yale University Press, 1964), pp. 77–78—noting that the actual enforcement of strict liability regulations depends upon the convenience of the prosecutor. LaFave, chap. 5, notes that because of limited resources, police may decide not to arrest when an offense is regarded as trivial; when the conduct (say, a stabbing in a Negro neighborhood) is regarded as part of the culture of a particular subgroup; when the victim does not or will not request prosecution; or when the victim himself was involved in misconduct (say, the customer of a prostitute).

degree of population instability may increase the reliance on formal sanctions, the evidence presented in the case studies suggests that the most significant variables are within the departments—specialization of the traffic enforcement function, demands by the chief and commanding officers that ticket writing or courtesy to motorists be stressed, and so forth. Where the norms of the department reward active ticket writers, the police will respond with tickets; where norms are neutral or openly hostile toward traffic enforcement, ticketing will be low and only serious offenders will be cited.

Enforcement and Safety. Police organizations, as we have seen, vary in the extent to which their activities are directed toward the production of traffic tickets. What difference does it make? It is standard dogma in the literature of highway safety that accidents can only be prevented by a combination of the "Three E's"—engineering, education, and enforcement.[11] Daniel Patrick Moynihan has argued that traffic laws should be thought of in terms of accident prevention, rather than punishing "crimes," and thus that the administration of these laws should be left to public-health doctors and engineers, who would be better able than the police to judge the degree of intoxication, the adequacy of driver vision and reflexes, highway-construction methods, and automobile safety equipment;[12] but at present it is generally assumed that enforcement is a matter best handled by police forces. The executive director of the International Association of Chiefs

11. See, e.g., Phil W. Ellis, "Traffic Safety," *Traffic Quarterly*, XVII (January 1963), 133–144.
12. Daniel Patrick Moynihan, "Public Health and Traffic Safety," *Journal of Criminal Law, Criminology, and Police Science*, LI (May–June 1960), 93; and "The War against the Automobile," *The Public Interest*, no. 3 (Spring 1966), 10–26.

of Police confidently declared in 1964 that police forces are "the pivot upon which all traffic safety efforts should turn."[13] One traffic engineer states flatly, "It seems too clear to require discussion here, that traffic duties are a logical and even necessary part of the duly established law enforcement bodies, and that they should not be assigned to a separate agency."[14] To the extent that the police conduct studied here was *not* based on considerations of safety (as when the ticketed violation was not hazardous or when the officer was simply trying to fill his quota rather than to seek particularly hazardous locations or conduct), Moynihan's proposed reassignment of the traffic function would make sense.[15]

Going beyond the question of which agency should handle traffic-law enforcement, there is the broader question whether enforcement is at all relevant to traffic safety. Police Administrator O. W. Wilson, advocating a police index of ten traffic citations for each personal-injury accident in the city, declares that "violations, and consequently accidents caused by them, are decreased by enforcement. The presence of accidents is evidence of a need for enforcement, and their frequency is a measure of the amount of enforcement needed."[16] Analysts of highway accidents, however, are no longer sure that law violations are the major cause of

13. Quinn Tamm, "The Police: Pivot for Highway Safety Efforts," *Traffic Quarterly,* XVIII (April 1964), 251.

14. Wilbur S. Smith, "Widening the Traffic Enforcement Front," *Annals,* CCXCI (January 1954), 74.

15. It should also be pointed out, however, that police administrators feel that traffic control is vital to police work for *nonsafety* reasons; the power to stop cars for traffic violations gives the police an opportunity to question and search suspicious persons, frequently leading to arrests on nontraffic charges. On the use of the traffic stop to interrogate suspects, see LaFave, p. 187; and Donald M. McIntyre, Lawrence P. Tiffany, and Daniel Rotenberg, *Detection of Crime* (Boston: Little, Brown, 1967).

16. O. W. Wilson, *Police Administration,* 2nd ed. (New York: McGraw-Hill, 1963), p. 369.

accidents (the current view is that the hazard is increased when speed is too fast—or too slow—for road conditions[17]), and there is some evidence that enforcement rates have little influence on the rate of traffic violations or accidents.[18] Although my study focuses upon the enforcement rather than the accident side of the supposed equation, I noted in the last chapter that local ticketing figures were only slightly correlated with traffic fatalities, property-damage or personal-injury accidents, or insurance rates. It is possible that accident rates might go up if the police adopted a publicly known policy of complete nonenforcement of traffic laws, or go down if drastic penalties were instituted (such as mandatory suspension for speeding or the Bulgarian policy of a death sentence for a second conviction for drunken driving).[19]

17. Noted, with qualifications, by M. Earl Campbell, "Highway Traffic Safety—Is It Possible?" *Traffic Quarterly,* XIX (July 1965), 339 (emphasis added).

18. Arthur D. Little, Inc., *The State of the Art of Traffic Safety: A Critical Review and Analysis of the Technical Information on Factors Affecting Traffic Safety* (Cambridge: Arthur D. Little, 1966); Robert P. Shumate, *The Long Range Effect of Enforcement on Driving Speeds: A Research Report* (Washington: International Association of Chiefs of Police, 1960); A. B. Calica, R. F. Crowther, and R. P. Shumate, *Enforcement Effect on Traffic Accident Generation* (Bloomington: University of Indiana Department of Police Administration, 1963). The role of automotive engineering defects in traffic accidents is documented by Ralph Nader in *Unsafe at Any Speed* (New York: Pocket Books, 1966). The findings of Shumate and Calica et al. are questioned by the still incompletely analyzed results of "Operation 101," in which the California Highway Patrol found lower rates of traffic violations and accidents after a massive increase in the number of police patrolling a stretch of super-highway in California. See California Highway Patrol, Operational Planning and Analysis Division, "Operation 101: Final Report Phase I, Background and Accident Analysis" (Sacramento: California Highway Patrol, 1966, mimeo).

19. The Bulgarian penalties are noted in "Overseas Rules on Traffic Given," *New York Times,* December 27, 1964. The reputed effect upon accidents of the widely publicized 1955 Connecticut crackdown on speeding is strongly questioned by H. Lawrence Ross and Donald T. Campbell,

But no evidence was found to support the theory either that high ticketing will produce a low accident rate (thus yielding a strong *negative* correlation) or that high accident rates will cause the police to adopt a strict ticketing policy (thus yielding a strong *positive* correlation); little correlation was found in either direction.

Policymaking.[20] At the beginning of this book, it was proposed that police activities be studied through an analysis of policy formation in gray areas—areas in which the conduct being regulated by the police is neither clearly condemned nor clearly accepted by the general public. Most traffic violations fall within this category, and though the formal traffic laws are certainly clear, they are hardly supported by a strong public demand that the police apprehend, say, all drivers who run stop signs. My study has shown the wide variety of policies which results from police uncertainty as to the relative importance of traffic-law enforcement. As James Q. Wilson has noted regarding other aspects of "the police problem," the police are forced to develop their own bases for traffic action because they get none from the public—or, more precisely, because the instructions given by the public are ambiguous, inconsistent, or otherwise unenforceable.[21] In all probability, we must expect that the police will continue to be forced to develop enforcement policies out of a maze of

---

"The Connecticut Speed Crackdown: A Study of the Effects of Legal Change," in H. Lawrence Ross, ed., *Perspectives on the Social Order*, 2nd ed. (New York: McGraw-Hill, in press).

20. I wish to thank Kenneth M. Dolbeare and James Q. Wilson for their helpful comments on earlier drafts of this section.

21. James Q. Wilson, "The Police and Their Problems: A Theory," *Public Policy*, XII (1963), 189–216.

conflicting and excessive legislative demands. As Herman Goldstein and Frank J. Remington have noted,

> However great the legislative contribution may be, experience demonstrates that legislatures can never deal specifically with the wide variety of social and behavioral problems which confront police . . .
>
> Certainly there is no reason to expect that legislatures can be more effective with respect to the work of police than they were with respect to the task of the economic regulatory agency. The "administrative process" and administrative flexibility, expertise, and, most important, administrative responsibility are as necessary and as appropriate with respect to the regulation of deviant social behavior as they are with respect to other governmental regulatory activity. This seems perfectly obvious. Yet the common assumption has been that the police task is ministerial, perhaps reflecting an assumption that administrative flexibility and "the rule of law" are inconsistent. This assumption seems invalid. The exercise of administrative discretion, with appropriate legislative guidance and subject to appropriate review and control, is likely to be more protective of basic rights than the routine, uncritical application by police of rules of law which are often necessarily vague or overgeneralized in their language.[22]

22. Herman Goldstein and Frank J. Remington, "The Police Role in a Democratic Society," in President's Commission on Law Enforcement and Administration of Justice, *Task Force Report: Organized Crime* (Washington: Government Printing Office, 1967), p. 18. See also Herman Goldstein, "Police Discretion," *Public Administration Review*, XXIII (September 1963), 140–148. In "Administrative Problems in Controlling the Exercise of Police Authority," *Journal of Criminal Law, Criminology, and Police Science*, LVIII (June 1967), Herman Goldstein analyses various bases of

If we accept the conclusion that primary enforcement decisions must continue to be made by the police, the question remains whether "appropriate legislative guidance" can be offered. In part, this question arises from the assumptions underlying all traffic-law enforcement—but we have seen that the data on traffic accidents provide little basis for concluding that a strict enforcement policy will reduce accidents. Whereas a strict enforcement policy may serve other symbolic values, such as displaying to the public an image of police aggressiveness, safety alone does not seem to justify such traffic endeavors. Thus we are left with no empirical basis for choosing between state-wide uniformity in effective enforcement levels and the observed (Table 21) local option to set any desired enforcement policy.

More broadly, the Goldstein-Remington thesis raises the question whether the public *can* offer adequate supervision of police policymaking. As we have seen, the effective policies in each city result from intradepartmental judgments about enforcement

---

police misconduct and the likelihood that various suggested control mechanisms will be effective.

Cf. Joseph Goldstein, "Police Discretion Not To Invoke the Criminal Process: Low Visibility Decisions in the Administration of Justice," *Yale Law Journal*, LXIX (March 1960), 586–587 (emphasis in original): "The ultimate answer is that the police should not be delegated discretion not to invoke the criminal law. It is recognized, of course, that the exercise of discretion cannot be completely eliminated where human beings are involved. The frailties of human language and human perception will always admit of borderline cases . . . But nonetheless, outside this margin of ambiguity, the police should operate in an atmosphere which exhorts and commands them to invoke impartially all criminal laws within the bounds of *full enforcement*. If a criminal law is ill-advised, poorly defined, or too costly to enforce, efforts by the police to achieve *full enforcement* should generate pressures for legislative action. Responsibility for the enactment, amendment, and repeal of the criminal laws will not, then, be abandoned to the whim of each police officer or department, but retained where it belongs in a democracy—with elected representatives."

priorities, and elected officials intervene only to give such *ad hoc* instructions as "Watch the stop sign at Main and Central," or "Crack down on Elm Street speeders." Few public officials find it profitable to intervene in general traffic-policy formulation. In other areas, such as the enforcement of laws regarding violence, civil disorders, and property crimes, a high degree of police responsibility is produced by a clearer and more attainable set of instructions and by a higher level of public surveillance. Unlike the traffic situation, in which almost no one knows what policies the police are following, in these more serious offenses the police are subject to regular supervision from interest groups (such as the Chamber of Commerce, the American Civil Liberties Union, or the civil-rights organizations), bar associations, and the judiciary. If we wish to reduce irresponsibility among police forces in the handling of such poorly defined areas as traffic, gambling, or prostitution, it must come through a clarification of the purposes of police action and an intensification of public surveillance. Until a greater level of consensus and support is generated, the police are scarcely to be blamed for their varying responses to the problems of traffic policy and enforcement.

Appendix: Research Methods

This book grew out of a Ph.D. dissertation written for the Department of Government at Harvard University during the year 1964–65. The starting point was an attempt to locate an area or phase of law enforcement in which it would be possible to demonstrate substantial intercity variations in police practices. With the full cooperation of Registrar James R. Lawton and the staff of the Massachusetts Registry of Motor Vehicles, it was possible to compute the total number of traffic tickets written by every police force in the state and the recommendations (warning, Registry action, or court summons) made upon them. On the basis of the measures described in the introduction (tickets per thousand motor vehicles, per policeman, and per thousand population), it quickly became apparent that the state's traffic laws were being unevenly administered by local police forces.

My first attempt to investigate these differences centered on interviews with local police chiefs. During the months of December 1964 and January 1965, I interviewed approximately thirty police chiefs in eastern Massachusetts, using a semistructured schedule of questions. The questionnaire, lasting from forty to ninety minutes, covered a variety of aspects of traffic-law enforcement, including formal organization (number of men assigned solely to traffic duties, whether men were allowed to carry Registry ticket books, and so on), relations with local judges, general opinions regarding local traffic problems, and the extent to which patrolmen were encouraged to write traffic tickets. Whereas these interviews produced a number of interesting anecdotes (descriptions of the ticket-fixing system or of lazy or overzealous policemen), they did little to explain the already-known variations in rates of ticketing. In particular, the interviews elicited few reliable indications of ticketing policies, since no chief admitted that he pushed his men to write a quota of tickets and all chiefs declared that they felt traffic enforcement to be an important police assignment.

Abandoning the formal interview technique, I decided to concentrate on a smaller number of cities and to look for informal differences which might lie behind the similar responses to the formal interviews. Accordingly, the most active (Waltham and Cambridge) and inactive (Lynn and Malden) police departments in the Boston area were selected. In each instance, I began by interviewing the chief, stating that I was a graduate student at Harvard interested in his force's traffic problems. After lengthy (three to four hours, continuing over several days) interviews with each chief, I asked permission to talk with all men specifically involved in traffic-enforcement work. In each of the four cities, I spoke with all captains, sergeants, and patrolmen given regular traffic assignments. Interviews with the patrolmen were quite informal and casual (on street corners or in patrol cars) and lasted from one to four or five hours. Beginning with questions about the seriousness of traffic problems and the attitudes of drivers, interviews would then turn to the length of time the respondent had worked on traffic, whether superior officers had ever tried to increase or diminish their production of tickets, and how the system of ticket fixing worked in their city. All men interviewed, from chiefs down to patrolmen, were exceedingly cooperative, although attitudes toward other men (or officers) in the department or toward ticket fixing would emerge only late in each interview.

The interview process within each of the four police departments involved about eight to ten men—the patrolmen with regular enforcement duties (or the most active ticketers where there were no enforcement specialists) and all superior officers connected with traffic. Where possible, nontraffic personnel in each department were also interviewed, but the announced focus of my study made it awkward to venture far beyond those directly working with traffic. In summary, then, the interview process concentrated on those who were in fact involved in traffic work and permits no conclusions to be made about other members of each department. Furthermore, since an informal interview style was used to maximize rapport, no attempt has been made in this book to offer more than approximate descriptions of policemen's attitudes. Finally, it must be kept in mind that my presence probably affected the conduct of the men being interviewed, although patrolmen in high-ticketing cities would interrupt interviews to flag down and ticket violators while patrolmen in low-ticketing cities were likely to point toward an observed violator and comment that only more flagrant conduct merited ticketing.

A second phase of study in each of the four cities centered on interviews with men outside the police department—newspaper reporters, civic leaders, and elected officials. From five to fifteen such men were interviewed in each city. Using unstructured interviews lasting about an hour, each respondent was asked for his general opinion of the local police department and his impressions of departmental policies regarding ticketing.

Original and follow-up interviews with policemen and outside respondents, followed by writing up the case studies, consumed about one month in early 1965 for each of the four cities. Late in 1965, to generalize beyond the Massachusetts data, written questionnaires were sent to all police chiefs in American cities with populations over 25,000. Of the 696 chiefs, 171 did not respond, 13 responded without giving ticket information, 4 responded that their city had delegated traffic work to the county sheriff's patrols, and 508 (73 percent) replied with information about the size of the police department, pay scales, and 1963 and 1964 ticketing figures. Space in the questionnaire was allowed for explanation of marked differences between figures for the two years.

After ticketing rates were calculated for the 508 cities, accident rates from the National Safety Council and 1960 census data collected by Professor Robert R. Alford of the University of Wisconsin Department of Sociology were used in the correlation and regression analysis described in Chapter Seven. Computer time for this project was subsidized by a grant from the National Science Foundation to the University of Wisconsin Computing Center.

A final comment might be added about the feasibility of social-science research into police activities. The vast majority of police chiefs and patrolmen contacted during this study were exceedingly cooperative and even pleased to be interviewed. Only 25 percent of the U.S. chiefs failed to return mailed questionnaires, and only two Massachusetts chiefs refused to be interviewed. More typical was the response of one chief who said, "This is a very busy day; I can only give you an hour. Come on in." The critical factor for success in interviewing policemen is simply one of approach. Policemen, like anyone else, will become defensive if accused of dereliction of duty—"Why do you beat Negroes?" or "Why aren't you following Supreme Court interrogation requirements?" It is quite easy, however, without any significant loss of neutrality on the part of the interviewer, to talk with policemen about their problems, be they traffic, riots, prostitution, or gambling. Although a police department currently under attack for alleged corruption or ineptitude may turn away or mislead interviewers, most police departments seem to be available to social-science research.

Index

Publications of the Joint Center for Urban Studies

The Joint Center for Urban Studies, a cooperative venture of the Massachusetts Institute of Technology and Harvard University, was founded in 1959 to organize and encourage research on urban and regional problems. Participants have included scholars from the fields of anthropology, architecture, business, city planning, economics, education, engineering, history, law, philosophy, political science, and sociology.

The findings and conclusions of this book are, as with all Joint Center publications, solely the responsibility of the author.

Published by Harvard University Press

The Intellectual versus the City: From Thomas Jefferson to Frank Lloyd Wright, by Morton and Lucia White, 1962

Streetcar Suburbs: The Process of Growth in Boston, 1870–1900, by Sam B. Warner, Jr., 1962

City Politics, by Edward C. Banfield and James Q. Wilson, 1963

Law and Land: Anglo-American Planning Practice, edited by Charles M. Haar, 1964

Location and Land Use: Toward a General Theory of Land Rent, by William Alonso, 1964

Poverty and Progress: Social Mobility in a Nineteenth Century City, by Stephan Thernstrom, 1964

Boston: The Job Ahead, by Martin Meyerson and Edward C. Banfield, 1966

The Myth and Reality of Our Urban Problems, by Raymond Vernon, 1966

Muslim Cities in the Later Middle Ages, by Ira Marvin Lapidus, 1967

The Fragmented Metropolis: Los Angeles, 1850–1930, by Robert M. Fogelson, 1967

Law and Equal Opportunity: A Study of the Massachusetts Commission Against Discrimination, by Leon H. Mayhew, 1968

Varieties of Police Behavior: The Management of Law and Order in Eight Communities, by James Q. Wilson, 1968

The Metropolitan Enigma: Inquiries into the Nature and Dimensions of America's "Urban Crisis," edited by James Q. Wilson, 1968

Traffic and The Police: Variations in Law-Enforcement Policy, by John A. Gardiner, 1969

Published by The M.I.T. Press

The Image of the City, by Kevin Lynch, 1960

Housing and Economic Progress: A Study of the Housing Experiences of Boston's Middle-Income Families, by Lloyd Rodwin, 1961

Beyond the Melting Pot: The Negroes, Puerto Ricans, Jews, Italians, and Irish of New York City, by Nathan Glazer and Daniel Patrick Moynihan, 1963

The Historian and the City, edited by Oscar Handlin and John Burchard, 1963

The Federal Bulldozer: A Critical Analysis of Urban Renewal, 1949–1962, by Martin Anderson, 1964

The Future of Old Neighborhoods: Rebuilding for a Changing Population, by Bernard J. Frieden, 1964

Man's Struggle for Shelter in an Urbanizing World, by Charles Abrams, 1964

The View from the Road, by Donald Appleyard, Kevin Lynch, and John R. Myer, 1964

The Public Library and the City, edited by Ralph W. Conant, 1965

Regional Development Policy: A Case Study of Venezuela, by John Friedmann, 1966

Urban Renewal: The Record and the Controversy, edited by James Q. Wilson, 1966

Transport Technology for Developing Regions, by Richard M. Soberman, 1966

Computer Methods in the Analysis of Large-Scale Social Systems, edited by James M. Beshers, 1968

Planning Urban Growth and Regional Development: The Experience of the Guayana Program of Venezuela, by Lloyd Rodwin and Associates, 1969

The Joint Center also publishes monographs and reports.